Curiosity

The Mental Hunger of Humans

Bernhard Kutzler

Curiosity: The Mental Hunger of Humans
Bernhard Kutzler

2nd Edition

Cover design © Hannes Kutzler, www.HannesKutzler.com
        (photo on cover by MJGraphics licensed from shutterstock.com)
Author photo on back cover by Hannes Kutzler
Copy edited by Philip Yorke
Published by Dr Bernhard Kutzler, Scharnstein, Austria, www.BernhardKutzler.com

Original edition (German): *"Neugier: Der geistige Hunger des Menschen"*

ISBN paperback: 978-3-9504875-4-1
ISBN hardcover: 978-3-9504875-5-8
ISBN ebook: 978-3-9504875-6-5

Contents

1

This is the story of my exploration of curiosity. What made me explore curiosity? My curiosity, of course! I've always been very curious. Therefore, I became a scientist and worked over twenty years as a mathematician. But the world has so much to offer – I was way too curious to deal with mathematics for the rest of my life. So I often explored other topics. Ultimately, I ended my career in 2009 and began to explore consciousness, human behavior, and human potential.

**

One day I decided to explore curiosity. I wanted to explore why I enjoy exploring.

> *Others have seen what is and asked: Why?*
> *I have seen what could be and asked: Why not?*
> *(Pablo Picasso)*

Pablo Picasso was one of the most curious people of the twentieth century.

> *I have no special talent. I am only passionately curious.*
> *(Albert Einstein)*

Albert Einstein was also one of the most curious people of the twentieth century. He has been my greatest inspiration since I was a teenager. I had my brother paint a portrait of Einstein on the hood of my first car.

Einstein is considered one of the greatest science geniuses in recorded history. Picasso is considered one of the greatest art geniuses in recorded history. The power that drove both and created their unbelievable careers came from their insatiable curiosity. I wanted to find out about this power. How does it emerge? What role does it play in life? Why do some people seem more curious than others? Why does curiosity come in so many forms? And so on.

> *Every child is an artist.*
> *The problem is how to remain an artist once we grow up.*
> *(Pablo Picasso)*

> *Play is the highest form of research.*
> *(Albert Einstein)*

As children we are limitlessly curious and permanently explore the world by asking 'Why?' and 'Why not?' in countless ways with all our senses and listening for answers. This stops when we grow up. Why?

A child's ravenous curiosity leads to its joy in and deep satisfaction with life. In fact, curiosity is the key to joy and satisfaction at any age. Can anyone become truly curious again?

Read on to learn what I found out.

I tell the story of my exploration of curiosity as a soliloquy because research is exactly that. I ask myself questions. I find answers. I question my answers. I find better answers. By telling the story of my exploration as a documentation of my chains of thought and reasoning, the results become comprehensible. Moreover: Why not write a non-fiction book in this format?

2

What is curiosity?

We[1] could consult a psychology book.

There we won't find what curiosity *is*. We would only
find a description of the author's *perspective* of
curiosity. Curiosity is much more than can be
expressed with words.

That's true for everything. The best description of a
red wine cannot replace tasting it. The best travel
report about Hawaii cannot replace a trip there.

Let's explore curiosity ourselves.

How do we start?

By exploring the word *curiosity*. What does it mean?

According to the online Cambridge Dictionary, it is
"an eager wish to know or learn about something."

This definition is superficial and vague, and therefore
useless. What does it mean to 'know'? What is
'something'? What is 'eager'? Language is an
important tool for our exploration. We must use
words as precisely as possible. We can't base our

---

[1] I often speak to and about myself in the plural ... after all, I was born under the
sign of Gemini, so, in the end, I am two. And already Goethe wrote: *"Two souls
alas! are dwelling in my breast."* Moreover, using "we" seems appropriate for a
soliloquy.

exploration on approximate meanings. What is the original meaning of the word curiosity?

What do we mean by 'original meaning of a word'?

Language is alive, and the meanings of words are constantly changing. This makes every communication a challenge. It's hard to know what someone wants to convey based on what he or she says or writes.

Let's take the word 'monk' as an example. It usually refers to a man living in a monastery.

The online Cambridge Dictionary gives the following definition: *"a member of a group of religious men who do not marry and usually live together in a monastery."*

This definition is unsatisfactory. For example, it doesn't explain the words 'religious' and 'usually.'

In an oral conversation, you can ask. But with written text, you almost always have to guess what the author intends to express.

The original meaning of a word is defined by its roots. Typically, the roots are from an old language such as Latin or ancient Greek. Since these languages are no longer spoken, the meanings of their words don't change anymore. Moreover, the roots often provide deep insights into the essence of what they denote.

The word *monk* originates from the Greek word *monakhos*, which means *"solitary."* Its root is the Greek word *monos* (= *alone*).

Therefore, the original meaning of the word monk is
a person who lives alone – regardless of gender and
whether he or she is religious.

We find the origins of words in etymological
dictionaries.[2]

> The word *curiosity* originates from the Latin word
> *cure*, which means *"care."*

Caring for something means focusing on it and doing
something for it – such as when a mother cares for
her child. However, curiosity is more than caring.
Albert Einstein cared about what he was doing, but
the essence of his *"passionate curiosity,"* as he put it,
was more than caring.

> We could research the word in other languages.

Let's look at some. French: *curiosité*; Italian:
curiosità; Spanish: *curiosidad*; German: *Neugier*;
Dutch: *nieuwsgierigheid*; Swedish: *nyfikenhet*.

> The words in French, Italian, and Spanish are similar
> to the English word and therefore have the same
> Latin root *cure*. The words in German, Dutch, and
> Swedish also seem to have the same root(s). So it
> suffices to look at one of them.

---

[2] Our primary source for the roots of words is Douglas Harper's *Online Etymology Dictionary* (www.etymonline.com). At the end of this book is a Glossary with all word origins we researched throughout this exploration.

The German word *Neugier* comprises two parts: *neu*
(= *new*) and *Gier* (= *craving, greed*). It expresses the
"craving for something new."

> The German word *Gier* has the Proto-Indoeuropean
> (PIE)[3] root **gher-* (= *to desire, like*). This is a less
> intensive form of longing than is expressed by the
> words craving or greed.
>
> Both the German word *neu* and the English word
> *new* have the PIE root **newo-* (= *new*). This definition
> is circular and therefore useless.

Let's try a different route. 'New' is an adjective.
When is something considered new?

> A new car is a car that is fresh from a dealership.

How long is a new car new?

> When we buy a new car, it's still new to us after, say,
> a month. But for the car dealer, it is no longer new
> once we signed the purchase contract and registered
> the car.

How about 'new' when we buy a used car?

> For us, it is still a new car.

---

[3] From now on we use PIE as an abbreviation for 'Proto-Indoeuropean.'

So, new can have two meanings:
(1) comes fresh from production or has not yet been
used,
(2) comes fresh into our life.
What's the essence of the difference?

                The first is from the perspective of the object, the
                second is from our perspective.

In other words, new as an *objective* property and
new as a *subjective* property.

How long is a new car new to us?

                As long as it smells new.

When is the smell no longer new?

                When we no longer perceive it as a new smell.

In other words …

                When we got used to it.

When we got used to our new car, we no longer
think of it as new. *Familiarization* kills newness. What
kind of newness is meant by the word
curiosity/Neugier?

                A curious person desires something that is new to
                him or her. Therefore, curiosity is about the
                subjective new.

Since the subjective new is the unfamiliar, the
unknown, curiosity/Neugier refers to a *"desire for
something one does not know or is not familiar with."*

We must keep in mind the aspect of caring from the English word curiosity. Einstein not only *desired* to find new knowledge about the universe, he *cared* about finding it.

To care about something means to give it your attention and to do something for or with it.

Desire is passive. We could sit motionless in a chair for an hour and desire something. Care is active. Care acts to get what desire seeks. This makes care the source of the power of curiosity.

**

Are people curious in this sense?

Hardly anyone is curious in this sense. People are creatures of habit.

But they desire new clothes, new cars, new phones, new vacation destinations, etc.

But it should not be *"too much"* new. The new dress should be new, but in the familiar style. The new car should be new, but of the familiar make. The new cell phone should be new, but everything from the old phone should be transferable, so you can keep using it. And even if someone buys his or her first car, computer, or cell phone, the motive is usually not true curiosity.

Many people buy a product because it is fashionable.

Regarding the central themes of life, people want to
keep what they have. They want to keep their
familiar lives.

What are the central themes of life?

One is partnership. Many people stay in a
partnership, even if it is fraught with strife or
indifference. They stay because they are afraid of the
changes a breakup would bring.

We know that from experience.

Another central theme of life is work. Most people
have a career that doesn't suit them. Either their
work doesn't fulfill them, or they experience
negativity with aspects of it. This makes their job a
burden, and they long for the workday to end before
it even begins.

What's behind the fear of change? Why does
someone stay in a career, even if it is not the right
choice?

The job brings money, and you need money to live.
Besides, what would the partner, the parents, the
friends, or the neighbors say if you quit your job? It is
not always easy to find a new one.

So it's about money and other people. What are
these two reasons really about?

Security and social acceptance.

Why do people remain in unsuitable partnerships?

Without a partner there is loneliness – and for most
people that is worse than quarreling or indifference.

Many people remain in an unsuitable career for fear
of being without money. And many people remain in
an unsuitable partnership for fear of being alone.
There is a similarity.

Partnership is also about security. It's about the
security that there is *someone* – no matter who.

For some people, a partnership is about financial or
economic security.

In the past, this was often the case for women, as
they were expected to raise the children and run the
household. This might still apply in some cultures.

A new partner/no partner or a new career could be
so much better than the status quo. But most people
are not curious enough to allow the fundamentally
new into their lives . Or they are too afraid to start
something new.

Yet many people feel that the status quo is not good
for them either and therefore crave a change.

An outlet for this craving can be *temporary* changes.

Such as vacations.

Or adultery. Or sick leave. An illness could be
simulated ... or caused by a life situation. In the latter
case, the psyche has arranged for a change.

We've had this experience. At the age of 20, we
worked as a software engineer. We didn't like the job
and did it only for the money. After a while, we got
sick. We were on sick leave for weeks, with fever and
unclear symptoms. After we quit the job, we got well
quickly.

**

Let's start with the question: Is curiosity natural?

How can we find out?

Let's look into nature. Where in nature do we see
curiosity or, rather, a behavior that *appears* as
curiosity?

When animals explore their environment, they
appear curious.

Does the term 'curiosity' apply to animals after all?
Do animals care? Do animals desire something new,
ie something they are not familiar with?

Why do we doubt?

The art of truly curious research is not to take
anything as certain, no matter how certain or
obvious it may seem. Einstein's research is a prime
example. He questioned the seemingly obvious: the
nature of space and time. And his curiosity paid off.
He found that the nature of space and time differs
from what everybody believed.

Back to animals. Why do animals explore their
environment?

       Maybe they are permanently searching for food.

That would make sense because in nature there is no
guarantee for a next meal.

       We just observed a housefly. It landed on our arm
and immediately began to suck up something with its
proboscis. It seemed to feed. When we moved our
arm, it flew away. Seconds later it landed again and
continued to feed.

There is something wrong with this explanation.

       Being curious means questioning everything. Do we
also question our own findings?

There are a thousand ways to err. There are a
thousand ways to persuade ourselves. Only what has
been questioned and tested over and over and
passed all tests has a *chance* of being true.

       Being curious is pretty strenuous!

With our emphasis on the word 'pretty.'

       What's wrong with the explanation *"permanent
foraging"*?

Animals spend a lot of time searching for food, but
there is more to their lives than food. Yesterday we
hiked up a mountain. Sitting on the summit, we
observed six flying ravens. They took advantage of
the thermal updraft to soar higher and higher. They

seemed to enjoy performing their flying skills. It was
beautiful to watch them. Also, a housefly often flies
around a room for minutes without landing and
feeding. If animal life was only about feeding, flying
would be a method to get from A to B as quickly as
possible. But observations of nature suggest it's
more than that.

> Some birds not only fly, they also sing – and there
> seems to be no connection between singing and
> feeding.

The daily routine of a songbird comprises feeding,
flying, and singing. What about other animals?

> A housefly feeds and flies. A wolf feeds and runs. A
> fish feeds and swims. All animals feed and perform
> their specific sensorimotor skills. They do for what
> they have the tools.

When we move from A to B, there are two possible
reasons. Either we need to get to B, such as to meet
someone, or we move to stay or become fit.

> It's the same with animals. Either a bird flies to fly, or
> it flies for a purpose such as feeding, escape,
> migration, or mating.

Talking of which … what is the purpose of mating?

> Survival.

What is the difference between feeding and mating
regarding survival?

> Feeding serves the survival of the animal, mating
> serves the survival of the species.

Feeding is a biological necessity for the *animal.*
Mating is a biological necessity for the *species*. It is
noteworthy that mating weakens the mating
animals.

Mating can even be lethal. If a male mantis doesn't
leave the female quickly after mating, there is a good
chance he will be eaten.

Mating weakens *every* male, because he sheds
precious sperm tissue. It requires a lot of food and
metabolic work to rebuild the lost tissue.

Females are more vulnerable during pregnancy and
parental care. And they must find more food than
usual to feed their offspring besides themselves.

Bottom line: Feeding strengthens, mating weakens.

Nevertheless, animals mate. There must be
something that urges them to do so despite the risks.

There is an instinct to mate, just like there is an
instinct to feed.

Are both behaviors really a result of instinct?

Do we question what experts say?

We must, because we are passionately curious. We
don't believe what others say or write, no matter
who they are. We want to see and understand
ourselves. That's what true curiosity is about.

We did some internet research. Neither behavioral science nor psychology has an unambiguous definition of the term instinct.

So let's find out. We want to understand why an animal behaves the way it does.

Aren't we getting off topic?

No. We are in the middle of it. Biologically, we are animals. Therefore, part of human behavior is animal behavior. Because humans have minds, there is an additional level of behavior and everything is more complex. We want to know if human curiosity is natural. For this, it helps to understand how animals naturally behave.

What does the word instinct mean?

This word originates from the Latin words *in* (= *into*) and *stinguere* (= *to prick, goad*).

Therefore, the word instinct aptly denotes something that causes a motion or change. We call it a behavior.

Let's recap. What exactly are we trying to find out?

We want to find out if curiosity is natural. For this, we ask the more general question: What behaviors are natural?

When a lion feeds, it's natural. When a lion mates, it's natural. When a lion jumps through a hoop of fire, it's not natural. But in all these cases, there is something that causes the behavior.

So the question is: What makes an animal behave
the way it does?

> Every behavior is a motion – either an outer motion
> of the locomotor system or an inner motion of
> organs. According to physics, every motion/change is
> caused by a force. So there must be a mover behind
> any behavior.

And since every life form moves in one way or the
other, there must be a mover in every life form. We
could explore this force/mover, but that would
distract us from exploring curiosity. Therefore, for
now, we'll just give it a name.

> Let's call it *life mover*. This wording is neutral. The life
> mover causes the life form to behave in a way that
> keeps it alive.

Each life form has its specific survival behavior, for
which it has the respective tools. Survival behavior is
created by the life mover.

Feeding *is* a life-sustaining behavior. Therefore, it is
an expression of the life mover.

> What other behaviors does the life mover create?

We remember the ravens we saw yesterday.
Something made them fly in majestic circles. The life
mover makes a bird fly and sing, a fish swim, and a
mole dig.

> But why would the life mover create this behavior?
> What is the point of flying if it doesn't serve a
> purpose such as food or escape?

Fitness. If a locomotor system is not sufficiently used,
it degenerates. If a skill is not sufficiently performed,
it weakens. If there is no other purpose, the bird flies
to improve or at least maintain its flying skills.

Wouldn't a daily 10-15 minute exercise routine do?

Nature is very competitive. Only the fittest survive. A
wild animal needs the highest possible level of
fitness to maximize its chances of survival. Therefore,
it must keep all of its skills permanently at the
highest level.

Let's imagine a herd of gazelles being hunted by a
pride of lions. The least fit gazelle has the highest
chance of having no chance.

Likewise, the least fit lion has the highest chance of
having no chance.

Gazelles and lions "motivate" each other to stay as fit
as possible.

Why don't we call the life mover *life instinct*? It fits
well with the established term *survival instinct,*
which causes a life form to behave appropriately
when threatened.

We are not happy with this choice, because the word
instinct is used in so many contexts – both
appropriately and inappropriately. But let's try.

The life instinct makes the life form express itself
powerfully. It makes the life form
(1) nourish itself,
(2) develop and maintain its natural abilities at the
highest level, and
(3) defend itself when attacked.

What's the role of the life instinct in mating?

The life instinct has only one goal: survival. The life
instinct is the elemental force that keeps a life form
alive. Since mating weakens a life form, it may not
come from the life instinct. Mating could be a
biological program superimposed on the life instinct.

What do we mean by superimposed?

The life instinct is the basis of life. It is effective 24
hours a day. Programs are effective only when
activated; such as a computer program that needs a
start command. Animals mate only at certain times
of the year. There may be a biological program for
mating, which is activated, for example, by a season.
When a biological program is activated, it takes
precedence over the life instinct. This is what we
mean by superimposed.

A biological program makes the life form behave in a
way that may contradict the life instinct. We've
recognized that mating weakens an animal, and in
the worst case can be fatal. The biological program
'maternal care' also makes a mother defend her child
by risking her own life.

How about a lion that jumps through a hoop of fire?
Obviously, this behavior contradicts the life instinct,
which would make the lion flee from fire.

The lion must have been programmed to do this.
More common terms for programming animals are
conditioning and training. The resulting programs
override the life instinct and biological programs.

This provides a link to humans. Education does just
that: it plants behavioral programs.

**

We still don't like the term *life instinct*.

What's wrong with it?

The word instinct is "too much." We think of it like
the throttle of a car. The life instinct makes an animal
feed. What makes the animal stop feeding? Animals
don't feed until they can't feed any more.

Also, the flight exercises of a raven end before the
bird falls from the sky in exhaustion.

There must be a dosing mechanism. For feeding, this
is hunger. The animal feeds when it is hungry and
stops when it is no longer hungry.

What does the word hunger mean?

It is used in the sense of *"unease or pain caused by
lack of food."* It originates from the Old German
word *hungar* (= *burning sensation*), which has the PIE
root **kenk-* (= *to burn*). Hunger is a burning sensation
that is experienced as lack or craving.

A person who likes to sing experiences a hunger for singing. After singing for a while, the hunger disappears, and the person stops singing.

A songbird could also be hungry for singing. The ravens we saw yesterday may have been hungry for flying.

So the ideal word for the life mover is *hunger for life*.

A songbird is hungry for food, flying, and singing. A mole is hungry for food and digging. A fish is hungry for food and swimming.

Every animal is hungry for food and moving, with the type of motion being determined by the animal's locomotor system. Birds fly, fish swim, moles dig.

Some animals have an additional hunger, such as the hunger for singing in songbirds.

Singing is also a result of motion, namely the motion of air when exhaling. So the hunger for singing is a variant of the hunger for moving.

3

How do we transition to humans?

We look at those humans who are closest to nature.

Are we talking about children?

Yes. We have a son. Therefore, we have memories
that will help us in our exploration. What was our
son like as a baby?

He slept a lot. When he was awake, he looked
around and kicked his legs and arms. When he was
hungry, he cried until we fed him. After some time,
he began to crawl.

He was hungry for food and moving. Just like an
animal.

With much perseverance, he explored what he could
reach by crawling. He often put objects in his mouth
or grasped them with his hands – as long as he didn't
use them for crawling.

Next, he learned to walk.

Why does a human bother to learn to walk on two
legs? Not only is it a strenuous endeavor, but walking
on two legs is more dangerous than moving on four
legs. What is the purpose of walking upright?

Standing and walking on two legs has two anatomical consequences: The hands are free for grasping and the eyes are as high as possible for seeing. The higher the eyes, the farther you see.

The farther you see, the more you see. This suggests a connection with curiosity, because curiosity wants to find something new.

So, humans are animals that master standing, walking, and grasping, and for whom seeing plays an important role.

**

Back to our son. What came after he had learned to walk?

As long as he crawled, he explored everything on the floor. Standing on two legs expanded his field of vision, walking on two legs expanded his field of grasping. When he saw something new, he craved to grasp it.

This formulation contains two essential keywords: *"When he saw something NEW, he CRAVED to grasp it."* The CRAVING to grasp something NEW is the essence of the German word for curiosity, NEU-GIER. How would this craving be phrased from our son's perspective?

"I crave grasping."

A child's life begins with a craving for food and moving. The second step of its development brings a craving for grasping. What came next?

Our son learned to speak. When he touched an object or pointed at it, we said the word that named the object.

And he imitated us.

Over time, his "echoes" became more and more like what we had said. He was eager to name objects. He pointed, we named, he repeated. His vocal skills improved and his vocabulary grew.

Another craving had developed, the craving for naming. This was the third step after the craving for food and moving and the craving for grasping. What was the next step?

His craving for naming was enormous. Soon, grasping objects and pointing at them were not enough. If he didn't have our attention, he attempted to get it. He tugged at our clothes or made his desire known with his voice. As a baby, his voice demanded food. Now his voice demanded names.

Names are elementary mental food. What happens when a child learns to name a person with a word, such as *"mommy"*?

It can use its voice to connect with that person. And it can do so from a distance, and even without visual contact.

Grasping is a physical form of contact. Seeing is a sensory form of contact, which is also physical, because seeing is a physical sense. Naming is a non-physical, a mental form of contact.

The word *"mommy"* establishes a mental connection with a person who bears this name.

This marks the beginning of thinking.

With words like 'tree,' things become more complex because there is not just one tree. Many objects – all trees – have the same name.

Ambiguity was an issue already with our son's two grandfathers. To distinguish them, one was named *"Vati-Opa"* (*"Daddy-Grandpa"*), the other was named *"Großer Opa"* (*"Tall Grandpa"*).

Obviously, this method doesn't work for trees because there are too many. By using the word tree as a name for many concrete objects, it becomes an abstract term.

The word *abstract* originates from the Latin words *ab* (= *away from*) and *trahere* (= *to draw*). The abstract remains when the concrete is drawn away – such as the concrete tree.

Names and abstract concepts are the starting point of comprehending.

The word *comprehend* originates from the Latin words *com* (= *with, together*) and *prehendere* (= *to catch hold of, seize*). Comprehending is a mental grasping. By using a name or an abstract term, you grasp something mentally.

Comprehending is the next stage in the mental development of a child. Comprehending begins with naming and grows in parallel with the development of language.

What was next in our son's development?

> Whatever he grasped, he explored more and more skillful with his hands. With infinite patience, he pushed and pulled on objects. He was fond of objects with moveable parts. He took many of them apart.

> Words turned into simple sentences. Simple sentences turned into complex sentences. The simple question *"What is this?"* turned into *"Why"* something is the way it is. Our son tirelessly asked questions. Helping him name objects was easy. Explaining why things are the way they are was often exhausting.

A child is ravenously curious. The questions it asks aloud are just the tip of the tip of the iceberg. Most of a child's questions are silent. By playing with an object, pushing or pulling it, or taking it apart, the child asks the object 'why' it is the way it is. In its play, the child explores the world, asks thousands of 'why' questions, and listens for answers with all senses.

How did we deal with the questions that our son asked aloud?

> Even though, compared to his silent questions, he only occasionally asked aloud, it seemed to us as if he was asking aloud permanently.

This showed how passionately curious he was. Like any child, our son was totally focused on exploring the world.

> When we didn't know an answer or when we were tired, we sometimes gave useless answers like *"because that's the way it is."*

Such answers dampen a child's curiosity.

> When we just wanted some time for ourselves after a long and tiring day, we occasionally even gave answers like *"stop asking so many questions."*

Such answers are a dagger to a child's curiosity! If a child hears this repeatedly, it will eventually stop asking.

> One day we sat on the couch with our son and watched TV. We saw a children's program that was rated for his age. He kept asking questions related to what he saw on the screen. While we answered, we missed part of the story. So after a few minutes, we asked him to stop asking and just watch the show. That's what he did from then on.

Our son was limitlessly curious. What he saw on the screen triggered his curiosity and asking aloud was the only option he had, because he could not touch or otherwise interact with what he perceived. A child can ask silent questions with its hands, mouth, and nose. But when it only sees or hears something, it must ask aloud. By asking our son to just watch and not ask any more questions, we had put yet another damper on his natural curiosity.

> This means: A child who watches TV without a person to answer questions learns to absorb information without reflecting on it – instead of interacting with the world and asking questions.

It becomes an uncritical consumer.

Back to answers like *"because that's the way it is"* and *"stop asking so many questions."* Why did we give such answers?

Because we didn't know the answer – or had no time.

"Having no time" is a really lame excuse. Every person has 24 hours available every day. The question is how we *use* the 24 hours. If you subtract sleeping time, working time, eating time, etc, some hours are left. Is it more important to watch the TV news or to answer the child's questions? The truth is, we didn't *want* to devote our time to our son's questions, or more accurately, we didn't *choose* to do so.

Who is that honest with themselves?

When we didn't know the answer, we could have said: *"I don't know the answer, but let's find out together."* We could have shown our son how to find answers.

Why didn't we do that?

Because we weren't truly curious anymore. Otherwise, our son's curiosity would have "infected" us. Every child is truly curious and truly curious people inspire each other.

Why were we no longer truly curious?

Because our parents stopped us from asking questions when we grew up. The reason for this was that our parents were no longer truly curious, because their parents had discouraged them from asking questions when they grew up. Stifling true curiosity is a pattern that has evolved over thousands and thousands of years. People, without knowing, pass it on from generation to generation as a rather unfortunate "mental heritage."

**

Does the fourth step, the craving for comprehending, complete the development of curiosity?

No, there is a fifth step. How does a child ask an object why it is the way it is?

It takes the object, pushes and pulls on it, and eventually deconstructs it into parts.

What else does a child do besides taking objects apart?

It puts objects together. It constructs. It piles up stones. It builds sand castles. Drawing is also construction, a construction of points, lines, curves, shapes, and colors.

What questions does a child ask by constructing?

"What is possible?"

You could also say: *"Why not?"*

The questions 'Why?' and 'Why not?' express the craving for comprehending and creating. Deconstructing is a central technique of comprehending, constructing is a central technique of creating.

Our son had a strong craving for creating that he lived out with building blocks.

Behind this was his ravenous curiosity, ie the
childlike version of the force that produced the
careers of Einstein and Picasso.

This is true for every child who lives in a supportive
environment.

4

Let's summarize the steps of a child's development.

> At the beginning of its life, a child craves food and moving. After that comes a craving for grasping, then a craving for naming, which turns into a craving for comprehending. The crowning is a craving for creating.

We saw the craving for food and moving in animals and recognized it as an expression of their hunger for life. This craving is *physical hunger for life*. The cravings for naming, comprehending, and creating are expressions of the *mental hunger for life*. They are specific to humans because they may require human languages. A human's craving for grasping is an expression of a mixture of physical and mental hunger for life.

> The mental hunger for life shows as *true curiosity*.

Children obtain joy of and satisfaction with life by satisfying their mental hunger (their true curiosity).

> There must be more than mental hunger. A cow feeds on grass, a lion feeds on meat. No matter how hungry a cow is, it will not become a carnivore. Since the physical appetite makes a life form choose the food, there must also be a mental appetite.

The mental appetite can be seen in children. One child is attracted to animals, another one is fascinated by the starry sky, a third one loves minerals, while a fourth can't let go of its drawing tools.

What is the purpose of hunger and appetite?

Physical hunger and appetite serve healthy physical
growth.

Then mental hunger and appetite serve healthy
mental growth.

When does an animal's physical hunger end?

When it dies.

Does hunger decrease during life?

It decreases during the last few days of approaching
death.

Likewise, every human remains mentally hungry,
lifelong.

How does the mental hunger (true curiosity) show in
an adult?

Naturally, it would be an advancement of the child's
craving for comprehending and creating. However,
most adults today are much less curious than
children. This shows that there is something wrong
with humankind.

Are there adults with an advanced form of true
curiosity?

Albert Einstein, Pablo Picasso, and Nikola Tesla spent
their lives exploring the world with the passion we
know from children. All three were truly curious –
with varying appetites. Einstein indulged in thought

experiments in physics, Picasso indulged in creating
artworks in ever new art styles, and Tesla indulged in
inventing electric devices.

Studying truly curious people can provide valuable
insights into true curiosity. There are many
biographies and documentaries available about
Einstein, Picasso, and Tesla, which makes them
accessible role models.

Another aspect is that their passionately curious
explorations changed the world. This shows the
enormous power of curiosity.

These three men shaped the twentieth and early
twenty-first century. Most of today's designs in
fashion and architecture are based on Picasso's art.
Global timekeeping, GPS, and space travel are based
on Einstein's research. The world's electrical power
systems and all wireless technology – radio,
television, remote controls, cell phones – are based
on Tesla's inventions.

How does Einstein's Theory of Relativity relate to a
GPS?

A GPS receives signals from satellites orbiting at an
altitude of about 12,550 miles (20,000 kilometers).
The position of the GPS can be calculated from these
signals. The Theory of Relativity states that time runs
differently in a satellite than on earth. This difference
is only a few microseconds per day, but this tiny
difference must be considered in order to calculate
the position of the GPS with an accuracy of three to
four feet.

Do we know anything about the curiosity of these
three men as children?

Yes, from their biographies. Einstein was four or five years old when he received a compass from his father. The behavior of the compass needle didn't fit his understanding of the world. Young Albert wondered *why* the compass needle behaved the way it did.

Picasso was passionate about drawing from a very early age. Young Pablo's first word allegedly was *"piz,"* which is a shortening of the Spanish word for pencil, *"lápiz."*

Tesla grew up in a small house surrounded by nature. He spent a lot of time with a cat named Macak. Nikola was four or five years old when, while petting the cat, he observed that the hairs of its fur glittered, sparkled, and crackled when he approached the fur with his hand. He asked his father about this phenomenon. The father had no answer, but suspected a connection with the lightning during a thunderstorm. Young Nikola wondered, *"Is nature just a big cat?"*

> Perhaps many children feel similar when holding a compass in their hands, observing electrostatic phenomena, or experiencing something else that doesn't fit into their view of the world.

Remarkably, Einstein, Picasso, and Tesla had childhood experiences that matched their later life topics. Tesla became an inventor in electricity, and the generation of lightning was his trademark. Picasso became a painter. Einstein became a physicist and discovered the Special Theory of Relativity with thought experiments about a moving magnet.

> This shows that the mental appetite manifests early in life.

We had an interest in science and research from an
early age. And we loved books.

One of our favorite books was a yellow 'Donald Duck'
book with instructions how to explore nature.

At twelve, we knew we would become a
mathematician.

But eventually we gave up that career.

We stopped working at the university and closed our
business. But in the genuine sense of the word, we
are still a mathematician, although we no longer deal
with numbers, variables, and geometric objects.
Instead, we deal with people and their behaviors.
The word *mathematics* originates from the Greek
word *mathema* (= *science*). In the genuine sense of
the word, a mathematician is a scientist – in
whatever field.

Our interest in humans also showed early. In sixth
grade, we had a biology teacher who lectured on
nutrition for the entire school year. We were so
fascinated by this topic that when we got home, we
told our mother what we had just learned. This
inspired her to look into whole food nutrition, read
books about it, buy a grain mill, and bake bread.

Our brother was passionate about drawing, painting,
and crafts. He made his first oil painting when he was
six years old. When he was twelve, he started filming
with a Super 8 camera. But because his school grades
were not "good enough," he was denied admission
to art school. Therefore, at sixteen, he began an
apprenticeship as a photographer. He became very
successful in this profession. He particularly loved
digital image processing because it offered him the

opportunity to live out his passion for drawing and
painting.

A few years ago he started filmmaking, which is his
artistic and professional passion now.

**

When you live your passion, work never stops.
Einstein, Picasso, and Tesla never stopped working.

Einstein continued his research until he died; his
research notebook lay beside his deathbed. A
discovery is not the end of research. It is a stopover
on a mental voyage that has no end. Since research
has no end, the truly curious researcher is never
done. Picasso's creative urge remained unabated
until his death. It is estimated that he produced
50,000 works of art. And Tesla, too, spent all his life
inventing.

We, too, can't imagine stopping to explore the world,
write books, and talk about our findings and
experiences. The thought of retirement just doesn't
occur to us.

So, one should do for work what gives you true joy
and satisfaction?

Is there a better way of life? Such a life is a treat!

This reminds us of an advertisement for coffee that
promises *"true satisfaction."*

Let's compare the satisfaction obtained from
drinking a cup of coffee with the satisfaction Einstein
obtained from exploring the laws of nature and
Picasso obtained from creating works of art. The cup
of coffee gives satisfaction for seconds or at most
minutes. Einstein's explorations of nature and
Picasso's creations of art gave these men a deep
satisfaction with life. Likewise, the pleasure we get
from exploring human behavior and human potential
is our satisfaction with life.

> So it's a matter of finding what gives you joy and
> satisfaction. Why is it so hard for people?

Because they learn that you have to work to earn
money. And they learn to seek for joy and
satisfaction outside of work.

> Because people are offered joy and satisfaction as
> consumer goods, they lose the ability to find within
> themselves the source of their true joy of and
> satisfaction with life.

> Speaking of consumption … one could consult a
> psychologist or career counselor. Can they give
> advice on what gives you genuine joy and
> satisfaction?

How would you know if the person knows their
craft? And even if you get the right answer, it doesn't
work.

> Why not?

Because you need the inner fire of enthusiasm that
apparently blazed fiercely in Einstein, Picasso, and
Tesla. This fire of enthusiasm ignites in the heart, not
in the mind. That's why it's not enough to be told.

You must *feel* it. The following anecdote describes this well:

> *A mathematics student asks his professor*
> *whether mathematics is the right choice for him.*
> *The professor replies: If you have to ask, then it is not.*

However, it's not that simple. Most people have lost touch with themselves, so they can't rely on what they feel.

But many people do believe in their gut feelings.

The problem with gut feelings is that they are influenced by programs. We feel what we've *learned* to feel.

This applies also to romance. When you fall in love with someone, it's usually a gut feeling thing. The phrase is *"having butterflies in your stomach."*

Your gut feeling makes those people appear attractive, with whom you can experience familiar patterns.

This explains why so many partnerships are repetitions of patterns people experienced as children.

This applies to partnership, career, and all other areas of life. Even in case people feel the "right thing," most don't have the courage to take the appropriate steps, because all too often they would clash with the interests of the social groups to which they belong.

Imagine we are walking on a path. We reach a fork in
the path. What do we do? Do we go right or left?

> We would make a spontaneous decision in this
> situation.

Next, imagine we are walking on the same path with
our partner. We reach the same fork. What do we
do?

> Ideally, we would make a spontaneous decision in
> this situation, just as we would if we were alone.

… without considering our partner! And of course,
our partner should do the same.

> What if our partner chooses differently?

This is what this thought experiment is about. If we
include a relationship with a partner, another
person, or possession in our decision, we cannot
choose freely.

**

> Is there some help for people who want to find out
> what work suits them?

There is a simple test to find out if your current work
is right for you. This test is the phrase: *"I don't live to
work, I work to live."*

> How is this a test?

It doesn't apply to Einstein, Picasso, and Tesla. In
fact, the opposite is true for them: They didn't work
to live; they lived to work. The same is true for us:
We don't work to live, we live to do the work we do.

> No wonder, because we really enjoy our work. For
> most people, their work is not satisfying, maybe even
> exhausting. These people strive for pleasure outside
> of work. They buy leisure pleasure with the money
> they earn from their work.

That's inefficient. If your work brings you pleasure,
you don't have to pay for it.

Although we enjoy our work, it is strenuous. But we
don't find the strain unpleasant. We enjoy it!

> There is strain with pleasure and strain without
> pleasure. What's the difference?

Strain with pleasure comes from fulfilling an inner
urge. Typically, peoples' hobbies are of this kind. If
you like to play tennis, a tennis match is a strain with
pleasure. Strain without pleasure occurs when you
follow a compulsion. This can be a job you are not
enthusiastic about. It can be a sporting activity that is
only a doctor's prescription.

> Following an urge can fulfill because it is liberating.
> Following a compulsion cannot be fulfilling because it
> is unfreedom.

Urge is pressure from inside. Compulsion is pressure
from outside.

5

How has our exploration of curiosity been so far?

It's been a real treat.

Our curiosity has sent us on a mental voyage where we experience mental adventures.

What is an adventure?

An adventure is *"an experience that differs from everyday life and has an uncertain outcome."* Einstein, Picasso, and Tesla went on mental adventures. None of them knew where his mental voyage would lead him.

You can take adventure vacations … even book them with a travel agent.

They may be labeled 'adventure,' but they are not adventures …

… because their outcomes are not uncertain.

A true adventure has no goal, and thus no planned end. For an adventure, you jump into the deep end without knowing what will come out of it. If you book a safari through the jungle or a trip to Antarctica or some other unusual, maybe even life-threatening place, everything is taken care of – including safety. Usually, you follow an itinerary and at the end you are on the plane booked to go home.

This seems reasonable, because people have a will to survive.

The will to survive refers to the desire to keep your *physical* life. But nowadays, people's physical lives are rarely in danger. At the end of a vacation, they sit in the plane to keep their *familiar* lives such as their careers.

Is there a connection with fear?

There are two types of *fear*. There is the fear of things that exist, and there is the fear of things that don't exist, things that are only imagined. The latter is often also called *anxiety*.

This word has the PIE root *angh-* (= *tight, painfully constricted*). Anxiety is experienced as a tightness.

Real fear is a biological reaction in the face of a real threat, such as from a tiger you come face to face with. Modern people experience existential threats only occasionally, such as when a car drives towards them while crossing a street. Nevertheless, most people have a lot of fears and anxieties. They are afraid that their *familiar* life could be damaged. They are afraid of changes that may come unplanned, such as losing a loved one, losing property, or career changes. People are afraid of losing control.

People want to control their lives?

They've learned to want to control their lives. Children don't control their lives.

We've recognized that people are creatures of habit
who want to keep key aspects of their lives, such as
partnership, career, and social groups.

On the one hand, they want to keep their familiar
lives, but on the other hand, their familiar lives
create boredom, stress, or other forms of
dissatisfaction. Therefore, they allow themselves
temporary exits from their familiar lives, so-called
vacations.

This word originates from the Latin word *vacatio*
(= *leisure, freedom, exemption, a being free from
duty*). The PIE root of this word is **eue-* (= *to leave,
abandon*).

The word *leisure* originates from the Latin word
licere (= *to be allowed*).

A vacation is time free from duty. When you need a
vacation, you experience your life as a duty. Isn't that
disturbing? A duty is compulsion from outside, which
is experienced as unfreedom. If you need a vacation
from your work, there is something wrong with what
you are doing as work. Einstein, Picasso, and Tesla
never needed a vacation from their work.

Imagine NASA is giving away three tickets: one for a
sightseeing flight on a space shuttle, one for a multi-
year expedition to Mars, and one for an exploratory
space flight with no set return date. You would be
alone on this third flight. You can apply for one of the
three tickets. The winners are chosen in a lottery.
How many applications would there be for each
ticket?

There would be countless applications for the space
shuttle flight because this is an exciting brief

vacation. For the Mars expedition there would be far
fewer applications because only a few people would
take a vacation of several years from their familiar
lives. For the lonely space flight with no set return
date there would be very few applications – if any; …
perhaps from people who have nothing to lose.

Usually, a person who has nothing to lose refers to
someone who is in a desperate situation. But it could
as well be someone who possesses nothing. If you
own nothing, you can't lose anything either.

Are we talking about material possession?

Not only. People who want to keep *their* life consider
their life their property. That's why they call it 'my
life' using the possessive pronoun *my*. There is so
much they consider theirs: my partner, my career,
my children, my parents, my friends, etc. They
believe that all this belongs to them somehow and
they want to keep it. The desire to keep something
inevitably creates the fear of losing it.

Does possession obstruct curiosity?

Let's look at the role possession played for Einstein,
Picasso, and Tesla, and the role it plays for children.

Children have no possession mentality – until they
learn it.

Einstein made his point:

Possessions, outward success, publicity, luxury –
to me these have always been contemptible.
(Albert Einstein)

Picasso wanted to *"live like a poor man with a lot of money."* By the end of his life he was very wealthy, but that was never his goal. After leaving his family and the prospect of a prestigious career as a traditional artist, he began as a very poor artist in Paris. He never strived for money. He valued money only for the opportunities it gave him as an artist.

After all, it speaks volumes that Tesla let go of a contract that would have made him a multi-millionaire. Instead, he gave away his intellectual property for next to nothing.

Truly curious people don't care about possession.

And vice versa, a person who strives for possession cannot be truly curious.

Why not?

Because gaining and protecting possession is a goal.
True curiosity has no goal.

We know people who work a lot with the goal of one day having enough money so that they can do what they *really* want to do.

These people postpone the satisfying of their mental hunger into the future. But this is an illusion. No one knows what will be in a few years or even months, and what personal and global circumstances will allow.

That's like planning to eat next week what you're hungry now.

Hunger and appetite are *now*. True curiosity and
mental appetite are *now*.

                                    **

                        How do we know if what we found out so far is true?

What is true?

                        We could explore what truth is.

If we want to know, we must explore it.

                        Some people say there is not only *one* truth, but
                        many.

What argument do they have?

                        Every person sees the world from their viewpoint.
                        This is *their* truth. And since every person is unique,
                        there are as many truths as there are people on this
                        planet.

What people see from their viewpoint is their
perspective – not the truth.

                        The word *perspective* originates from the Latin words
                        per (= *through*) and *specere* (= *to look at*) and means
                        "a way to look at something."

The view of a city from an airplane differs completely
from the view of the city when standing on a
neighboring hill, and the latter differs completely

from the view that someone has when walking
through the city.

From a neighboring hill you can see which is the
tallest building of the city, but not the shortest route
from the railway station to the church. For the latter,
you should use the bird's-eye view of a city map.

A perspective is neither right nor wrong. In a
situation it is more or less useful.

What do we see when we look at this tree?

We see those parts of the trunk and the crown that
we can see from where we stand. And no matter
where we stand, we don't see the tree's roots.

From where we stand, we have a perspective of the
tree. But this perspective is far from the truth of the
tree.

What is the truth of the tree?

Let's explore the word *truth*.

It has the PIE root *deru-* (= *be firm, solid, steadfast*).

This shows that truth does not depend on a
viewpoint. Truth is steadfast; it is something you can
trust in. Truth is firm and stable.

Then there is only *one* truth.

The one truth about the tree is the tree itself.

What is the truth about a person?

A person *is* their own truth.

Do people know their own truth?

People have a perspective on the tree. Likewise, they also have only a perspective on themselves.

**

In a book, we would not have found the truth about curiosity, but a description of the author's perspective.

But isn't this book also only a description of our perspective?

Yes – and yet it is more than that.

Because?

The truth about a tree is the tree itself. Therefore, to know the truth about a tree, you must *be* the tree.

Likewise, to know the truth about curiosity, you need to *be* true curiosity.

We must be truly curious – as passionately and ravenously curious as Einstein was, and as every child is.

We confirm that we are that curious.

This story about our exploration of curiosity is a documentation of our *being truly curious*. Therefore, this text *can* be an inspiration to be truly curious.

You cannot read about truth. You can only *be* the truth. Truth is beyond language.

> What is the difference between truth and knowledge?

Let's find out what the word *knowledge* means.

> This word has the PIE root **gno-* (= *to know*).

This doesn't help, because it is a circular definition.

> An archaic synonym of the word *know* is the word *wit*, which originates from the Old English word *witan* (= *to know*), which has the PIE root **weid-* (= *to see*), which is also the root of the German word *wissen* (= *to know*). *To know* means *"to see."*

We know what we see. Meaningfully, this refers to any form of sensory perception, not just visual sight; and it includes mental seeing, such as seeing something fictitious (imagining).

> Can we get knowledge from a book or a teacher?

If we read in a newspaper about a train accident in France, we *know* nothing about the accident. We can't know anything about it, because we haven't been there and *seen* the accident. We only know what is written about the accident in the newspaper, because we have seen this text with our eyes. This is an important difference that most people are not aware of.

Even the author of the newspaper article most likely
has not seen the accident but has only taken a text
from a news agency.

Knowledge is personal. A person knows what he or
she sees or has seen. No more and no less.

What about the knowledge you learn in school?

In school you learn perspectives. For example, many
scientists say that our universe is about 14 billion
years old and began with a Big Bang. But that is not
knowledge in the original sense of the word …

… because no one has seen a Big Bang.

Most scientists today accept the *perspective* that the
universe is about 14 billion years old and began with
a Big Bang.

The formulation *"according to the latest scientific
findings"* shows that today's scientific perspectives
differ from the perspectives science had yesterday.

And almost certainly, future scientific perspectives
will differ from today's.

By the way: The word *theory* is akin to the word
perspective. It originates from the Greek word
theoria (= *a looking at, viewing*), which has the roots
thea (= *a view*) and *horan* (= *to see*).

Therefore, the Theory of Relativity is only a
perspective.

Yes. Like a perspective, a theory is neither right nor wrong. Like a perspective, a theory is only more or less useful in a situation. Theories in physics are judged by their *usefulness* for describing and predicting the universe's behavior. Einstein's Theory of Relativity explains and predicts phenomena that cannot be explained or predicted by other theories. This makes it more useful than other theories. A confirmation of a theory is about its *usefulness*. Einstein was well aware of this, as the following quote documents:

> *Whoever undertakes to set himself*
> *as a judge of truth and knowledge*
> *is shipwrecked by the laughter of the gods.*
> *(Albert Einstein)*

6

How do we recognize *true* curiosity?

Through the qualities focus, initiative, autonomy, and risk-taking.

What is *focus*?

This word is Latin and originally means *"heart, fireplace"*. Since 1796 it has been used in the sense of *"center of activity or energy."*

What is *initiative*?

This word originates from the Latin word *initiare* (= *to begin*), which is composed of the words *in* (= *into*) and *ire* (= *to go*). Initiative is the first step that must be taken before further steps can be taken; to take initiative means to be proactive.

What is *autonomy*?

This word originates from the Greek words *autos* (= *self*) and *nomos* (= *custom, law*). Synonyms are *self-government*, *self-dependence*, and *independence*.

What is *risk-taking*?

The word *risk* originates from the Italian word *riscare* (= *to run into danger*). Risk-taking is the courage to begin an undertaking without knowing what will be.

This is like an *adventure*.

Children focus on what they are doing. They are
constantly initiative (proactive), autonomous, and
willing to take risks. Children explore the world –
without ifs and buts.

This often causes stress for their parents. As a father,
we know this from experience.

That's how children are. Ravenous curiosity is their
very nature. Children have an enormous need for
autonomy. A child wants to do everything itself. It
wants to hold the spoon itself; it wants to walk up
the stairs itself. It wants to explore the world itself.

How about the three geniuses?

They were like children in many ways. They were
focused on their work. They were initiative. They
took enormous risks – financial, social, professional,
and health-wise. And they were autonomous. They
always wanted to find answers themselves. Einstein
was skeptical about the answers Newton and
contemporary physics had to his questions. Picasso
was skeptical about established art styles. Tesla was
skeptical about direct current, which was becoming
popular.

What comes out of true curiosity?

True curiosity makes us ask questions. The word
question originates from the Latin word *quaerere*
(= *to ask, seek*). The word *ask* has the PIE root **ais-*
(= *to wish, desire*). For a truly curious person, asking
questions (silently or aloud) is as strong a desire as
wanting food is for someone truly hungry.

True curiosity makes us explore what is by asking
'Why' – which leads to *comprehension*. And it makes
us explore what could be by asking 'Why not?' –
which leads to *creation*.

**

Let's look at the development of curiosity again.

> The first step is the craving for food and moving.
> The second step is the craving for grasping.
> The third step is the craving for naming.
> The fourth step is the craving for comprehending.
> The fifth step is the craving for creating.

Each of these steps develops something in us.

> The craving for food and moving develops and
> maintains the body.
>
> The craving for grasping develops the fine motor
> skills of the hands and indirectly supports the
> development of walking and standing on two legs.
>
> The craving for naming develops the voice and starts
> the development of the mind.
>
> The craving for comprehending and the craving for
> creating develop the mind.

The development of curiosity accompanies the
development of the three tools that make us unique
on this planet: hands, voice, and mind.

The human mind is truly exceptional. It is *the* human
tool and distinguishes us from animals. The mind is
closely related to consciousness. We've meticulously
explored consciousness for years and written a book
about it. There we explain what the mind is, what
purpose it serves, and how it works.[4]

The mind is a human's most powerful tool.

It makes us limitless.

For this, you must know how the mind works.

Einstein established one of the most superb feats of
intellect in recorded history. Using only his mind, he
conquered realms that no one had entered before.
But the potential of the mind is much greater than
what Einstein achieved with it.

Back to the three human tools. Hands and voice are
physical tools. The mind is a mental tool. What is
'mental'?

This word originates from the Latin word *mens*
(= *mind*).

This is a circular definition and thus useless.

In the book on consciousness, we explain what the
mind is, and we explain both the difference and the
connection between physical and mental. For this
exploration of curiosity, it suffices to interpret
mental as *non-physical*.

---

[4] See the chapter "Resources" for details about the book on consciousness.

Human hands are also exceptional on this planet.

No other life form has such a powerful grasping tool.
Apes also have hands with long fingers, but they lack
the long thumb, which is crucial for effective
grasping.

You can experience this with a simple experiment:
Simulate a short thumb by performing everyday
tasks, such as brushing your teeth, without using the
thumb's upper phalanx.

Our long thumb is a "anti-hand" for the other four
fingers. Together they make an effective pair of
pliers.

The Greek word for thumb is *anticheir*, which means
'anti-hand,' because the Greek word *cheir* means
"hand."

The human voice is also exceptional. No other life
form on this planet has such a powerful tool for
producing sound. It was the physical prerequisite for
the development of human languages.

What is the role of the hands and the voice
compared to the role of the mind?

The mind is the primary tool of humans. The hands
and the voice are the mind's handmaidens, so to
speak. The mind is mentally hungry. Its hunger is
satisfied with explorations that aim at
comprehending the world and creating in it.

Every child is doing just that.

In order to comprehend the world, we explore what
is – as expressed by the question 'Why?'. The central
technique is deconstructing, for which we use our
hands and our mind. Deconstructing with the mind is
called *analyzing*.

In order to create in the world, we explore what
could be – as expressed by the question 'Why not?'
The central technique is constructing, for which we
use our hands and our mind.

When several people work together to comprehend
the world and create in it, they must communicate
about their thoughts and ideas.

> But only the truly curious people contribute
> constructively.

Therefore, truly curious people seek communication
with truly curious people. For this, they need a
language that allows the nuance necessary for a
mental exchange.

Such languages could only develop because the
human voice allows sufficient nuance of pitch and
volume.

**

> Let's talk about the importance of the mental
> exchange between truly curious people.

Both Einstein and Picasso had small groups of trusted
friends whom they met regularly. In these groups
they talked about topics relevant to their work.
Einstein's group was called *Akademie Olympia* and

comprised Einstein, Maurice Solovine, and Conrad
Habicht. Picasso's group was called *La Bande à
Picasso* and had changing members, mostly artists.

What are the roles of books and journals?

They allow communication between people that
cannot talk to each other because, for example, they
don't live – or have not lived – at the same time.
Einstein knew the relevant publications of his
predecessors and contemporaries. The works of the
Dutch mathematician and physicist Hendrik Antoon
Lorentz and the French mathematician Henri
Poincaré were his most important inspirations.

Picasso, too, was inspired by Poincaré. This
happened through the mediation of the French
mathematician Maurice Princet, who was a member
of the *La Bande à Picasso* for some time.

Einstein revolutionized space and time in physics.
Picasso revolutionized space and time in art.
Poincaré paved the way for both.

Tesla also revolutionized space and time. It is thanks
to his inventions that today we can go almost
anywhere on this planet in comparatively short time
and that we can connect with almost any part of the
world almost instantaneously. Tesla's inventions
have turned the world into a global village.

In what way did Picasso revolutionize space and time
in art?

Before Picasso, artists produced works of art that
copied reality.

Most of the paintings of old masters look like photographs.

Picasso created paintings where the proportions didn't match. For example, he painted a head either too large or too small compared to the rest of the body. This is nothing more than a change in the geometry of space.

What about time in Picasso's art?

Realistic paintings are snapshots – just like photographs. They have no temporal dimension because the moment has no length. The art of moving images, the *movies*, included time into visual artwork.

Picasso created pictures in which objects were shown from multiple perspectives. For example, he painted parts of a head as seen from the front, other parts as seen from the side. With this, Picasso portrayed time because it takes time to see the head first from the front and then from the side. In a way, he packed a movie into a picture.

Distorted proportions and mixing of perspectives are often seen in children's pictures.

Adults are trapped by space and time. Children see the world beyond space and time.

This freedom is lost somewhere on the way from child to adult.

**

The cravings for naming, comprehending, and creating develop the mind. How can this be imagined?

When a child learns to name objects and thus learns to speak, it develops a *mental world*.[5]

Let's say, a child's first word is *"mommy."* This creates in the child's mental world the mental mother as a mental copy of the real mother. When it learns the word *"daddy,"* the mental father is added to this world. And so on.

This is like what you can do with a video camera. The camera's recording is a digital copy of the real world. You might film a portrait of the mother, then a portrait of the father, etc. The collection of the recordings makes the digital video world.

A person's mental world is much more complex than a digital video world. The child is permanently in recording mode, so to speak. It records on multiple channels, one channel for each sense.

What are the roles of parents and other caregivers?

They are key. They influence the development of the child's mental world simply by being around. The child is permanently recording (= learning) with all senses. Everything someone says, does, doesn't say, or doesn't do in the child's presence becomes part of the child's mental world.

----

[5] The *mental world* corresponds to what we call the *human program* in the book on consciousness and the *human box* in our book "Being Free: Get Out of the Box." We will come back to this in Chapter 10.

This gives *"being an example"* a whole new meaning.

In the first years of life, a child is surrounded primarily by its parents, perhaps only one parent, perhaps siblings. Therefore, a child's mental world starts as a mixture of parts of the mental worlds of these people. Over time, this world is expanded by parts of the mental worlds of the people the child spends time with, such as grandparents, uncles, aunts, cousins, friends, neighbors, teachers. The more time the child spends with a person, the more of that person's mental world flows into the child's mental world.

The mental world includes previous generations.

A child's mental world is primarily determined by its parents' mental worlds. The parents' mental worlds were primarily determined by the grandparents' mental worlds, extended by the parents' life experiences. The grandparents' mental worlds emerged from the great-grandparents' mental worlds, extended by the grandparents' life experiences. And so on. Ultimately, a child's mental world is a mixture of the life experiences of countless generations.

If a child has a friend with whom it spends a lot of time, the mental world of the friend also influences the child's mental world.

And vice versa. And since the best friend's mental world combines the life experiences of the best friend's family and predecessors, a lot of mixing of mental worlds happens. In fact, this is true whenever people interact socially.

This is like a computer virus.

It is much "worse" than a computer virus, because
the "infection" happens simply by perceiving
someone. You even get infected by fictional
characters such as from books, movies, and
computer games. In these cases you take on parts of
the mental worlds of the authors, directors, and
programmers. There is nothing you can do about it.
There are no "antivirus programs."

> But since we are humans, we can *choose* what we
> consume and if and with whom we interact socially.

> What happens when the child perceives (and thus
> records) something that is already part of its mental
> world?

The more often a child perceives/records something,
the more significant and thus powerful it becomes in
the child's mental world. Repetition is a strong
programming mechanism.

> What happens when the child experiences
> discrepancies, such as receiving praise and blame in
> the same situation?

Everything becomes part of the mental world, and
nothing is ever lost. When a child experiences both
praise and blame as consequences of an action, the
result is doubt or tension.

> We did that to our son. We often praised him for his
> curiosity. But sometimes we rebuked him with
> phrases like *"stop asking so many questions."*

This taught our son that his curiosity can be both
right and wrong.

What is the role of a child's questions?

The questions express the child's mental appetite.
They determine the direction in which the mental
world grows.

64

Is there anything else that influences the mental
world?

Everything a child comes into contact with becomes
part of its mental world. Today, media play a major
role: television, internet, movies, video, computer
games, and music.

But this is not limited to childhood.

The underlying "mechanisms" are effective
throughout life.

Therefore, *our* mental world also grows permanently
through our social contacts.

As well as through our media consumption, which
includes newspapers, magazines, books, and social
media. We reflect on this in the book on
consciousness and in the book *"Being Free."*

**

What happens when the child stops asking
questions?

Curiosity is mental hunger. Naturally, a person
remains hungry throughout life – both physically and
mentally. Naturally, a child would never stop asking

questions. Therefore, every adult would continue to
ask questions all the time.

> But even if the child is conditioned to stop asking
> questions, its mental hunger must still exist. Mental
> hunger doesn't disappear, just like physical hunger
> doesn't disappear. How does mental hunger show in
> people who have been conditioned to not ask
> questions anymore?

Let's find out.

7

Most parents support their child's development in the first years of life. But when it gets older, parental support decreases. Not only are children supported less, their further growth is often obstructed. As a result, children eventually stop exploring the world.

Are there obstructions other than requests such as *"Stop asking so many questions."*

There are situations that seem meaningless, but have a devastating effect on true curiosity and beyond.

Let's imagine a child playing. It is totally absorbed by its play, which is a passionately curious exploration of the world. It is noon, and a parent calls the child for a meal. The child responds it is not hungry. But it must obey. It must stop its play and eat.

Is it really not hungry?

Yes – because it was fully focused on its play. Let's imagine Picasso painting a picture. It is noon and his wife shouts: *"Pablo, food is ready."* Can we seriously imagine that Picasso immediately drops brush and palette, rushes to the dining table, and pounces on the meal?

We know that this is a rhetorical question.

Certainly Einstein never interrupted a chain of thought because lunch was served. Certainly Tesla never dropped his tools because the church bells announced noon.

We remember situations when we "forgot" a meal because we were absorbed by an activity. But we didn't forget to eat. You can't *forget* to satisfy your hunger. Hunger is a natural force that cannot be ignored.

Every baby is living proof.

However, you can forget mealtimes. But mealtimes are not natural. In nature, food intake is determined by hunger – not by the clock. Mealtimes are a human invention. Sticking to mealtimes is like a lion jumping through a hoop of fire. It's an unnatural behavior.

Back to the image of the playing child. The child is curious and satisfies its mental hunger with its play. In the midst of it, the child is called to lunch. It is torn out of its play, ie out of its mental feeding. It is forced to eat, although it is not hungry. This creates several disturbing programs.

The child must stop its curious exploration of the world. It *learns* that its curiosity is wrong.

The child is torn out of its *focus* – with focus being an essential aspect of true curiosity. The child *unlearns* to stay focused. Later, as adults, we must learn again to stay focus ...

The child must eat even though it is not hungry. The child *learns* to follow external signals rather than its own natural signals.

The child *unlearns* autonomy, which is also an essential aspect of true curiosity.

The child *learns* that its feelings are worth less than
instructions given by others. It *learns* that it is worth
less than the people who give these instructions.

The child *learns* a feeling of inferiority.

Curiosity is mental hunger. The child is mentally
hungry, but not hungry for food. But it *must not* eat
mentally, instead it *must* eat physically.

The child *learns* to *try* to satisfy its mental hunger
with physical food (which doesn't work).

Because this happens repeatedly in this or similar
ways, these programs become stronger and stronger.
The result is someone who functions, consumes, and
feels inferior.

Eating at set mealtimes is a pattern that virtually
everyone learns – in virtually all cultures.

This conditioning may start with breastfeeding. Any
rule other than *"if and only if the baby is hungry"* is
an unnatural conditioning. Even if some mothers let
their babies choose breastfeeding times, they
eventually force them into the usual mealtime
schedule "breakfast – lunch – dinner."

Everyone adheres to mealtimes because they are
normal. Mealtimes are normal because everyone
follows them. No one questions this vicious circle,
therefore no one leaves it.

This is reminiscent of the story of a frog sitting in a
pot filled with cold water. The pot is slowly heated
until the water boils. As the water gets hotter and
hotter, the frog just remains sitting in the pot – and

dies. It is boiled alive, without fighting. If, instead, the frog is put into a pot filled with hot water, it will fight for its life. It will do anything to escape the hot water.

True curiosity is killed in countless infinitesimally small steps. Although ... it is not a killing, but a diversion. When a child learns to *try* to satisfy its mental hunger with physical food, the power of true curiosity is diverted, not killed.

This sheds new light on the worldwide increase in obesity.

The force of true curiosity cannot be ignored. If a force cannot act naturally, it acts differently. Every force finds a way to act. This is physics. Once a child has learned to use physical food as an alternative channel for mental hunger, it will substitute pseudo-curious explorations of the fridge for truly curious explorations of the world.

Is there evidence?

Food plays a paramount role in our society. This role goes far beyond satisfying the natural hunger for food. Some people crave large amounts of food, others crave a wide variety of foods. Carbohydrates and sweets play a prominent role because they satisfy faster than other food.

What role does food play for truly curious people?

A minor role. Truly curious people tend to eat too little rather than too much. If you lead a truly curious life, you also feed mentally and therefore may need less physical food.

We observe this in ourselves. When we are
passionately engaged in something, food is
unimportant; almost an annoyance. But when we
must perform a boring task, food becomes important
– and we tend to eat more than usual.

In such a situation, food becomes a distraction and a
substitute channel for obtaining satisfaction.

**

Are there other alternative channels for true
curiosity?

There are quite a few. Curiosity is mental hunger and
thus a longing for mental satisfaction. Anything that
satisfies can serve as an alternative channel. More or
less, this is anything that feels good.

Sounds like the pursuit of happiness.

Happiness … a big word. But it's nothing more than
feeling good.

**

What did we enjoy as a child?

We enjoyed collecting. We collected bottle caps,
matchboxes, and stamps.

Why did we collect exactly these things?

We followed examples. Our father collected stamps,
and one of our cousins collected bottle caps and
matchboxes. He was a few years older, and we
admired him.

Has our son collected anything?

He collected movies, which he recorded on VHS
tapes. He had a large collection with hundreds of
movies. He was very passionate about this collection
and invested a lot of time in browsing TV programs,
recording movies, and managing the collection.

Is collecting natural or learned? Do animals collect?

Some rodents and some birds gather food, either to
let it ripen or to have food for times when food is
hard to find. Some birds and some monkeys collect
shiny objects, which they seem to use for attracting
mates.

These collections serve biological purposes.

So, most human collecting is not natural?

Most human collecting is a human invention. It
becomes part of the mental world of a person and is
passed on to others. We have learned it from our
father and our cousin. Our son has learned it from
us.

What is the purpose of collecting?

It satisfies. You experience satisfaction when you find
a new item for your collection, when you look at or
manage the collection, and when you show the
collection to others. But these feelings are short-

lived – and that's the rub. If you want a collection to
give you good feelings regularly, you must regularly
add to it, look at it, manage it, or show it.

> Our father spent countless hours each year
> determining the value of his stamp collection
> according to the newly published collector's
> catalogue – down to the cent!

> Does collecting have any other meaning or
> relevance?

It is the gateway to possession.

> What do children collect?

In the past, children collected waste products like
bottle caps and used stamps; or objects they found
in nature, like rocks. Today, children mainly collect
items for which their parents pay directly or
indirectly, such as trading cards. Once a child is older
and receives pocket money, collecting turns into
buying.

> Don't people buy products when and because they
> need them?

Most of today's shopping is an *experience*, not a
necessity.

> A shopping afternoon in an air-conditioned mall is
> like a mini vacation. Even more so when it's
> uncomfortable outside, such as rainy, freezing cold,
> or very hot.

Furthermore, most shopping today is a form of
collecting. Shopping provides the four experiences of
satisfaction we've seen in collecting. Finding a new
product is as satisfying as proudly viewing, managing,
or showing one's collection of shoes, fashion,
technology, etc.

We are no stranger to this. We thoroughly enjoyed
buying books. It was almost impossible for us to walk
past a bookshop. So, over many years, a private
library had developed comprising several thousand
non-fiction books.

As much as we enjoyed buying new books and
looking at the huge book wall in our living room, the
downside was the immense amount of work we had
each time we moved to a new place …

**

How do we find the other alternative channels?

We continue to look at a child growing up. In this
way, we will find one alternative channel after the
other.

What else do children like to do?

They enjoy moving, ie sports.

Those are two different things. Moving is natural.
Every life form with a locomotor system is hungry for
moving. Sports are something else.

> The word *sport* originates from the Old French word
> *desport* (= *pleasure, enjoyment*), which is composed
> of the Latin words *des* (= *away*) and *portare* (= *to
> carry*), and thus means *"carry away."*

Sports, therefore, is a form of distraction. A sporting
activity *"carries you away"* – such as from worries.
Appropriately, 'sport' is also a colloquial word for a
person you can hang out with.

> There are not only physical sports but also mental
> sports. In English they are called *mental exercises*.
> The German word is *"Denksport,"* which literally
> translates into *"thinking sports."* For some time, we
> loved to play Sudoku.

Why?

> Finding a number and entering it into the Sudoku
> puzzle felt good. When the scheme was complete,
> we had a crowning experience of satisfaction.

Do we see the similarity to collecting?

> Yes. Sports – physical sports and mental sports – can
> provide satisfaction.

We enjoyed not only mental exercises ("thinking
sports") but also action sports.

> At 15, we began to play badminton. At 17, we
> switched to dance sports.

Why?

We enjoyed moving our body to music; we enjoyed
the exercise; we enjoyed the challenge of learning
new routines; we enjoyed perfecting our routines;
we enjoyed the fellowship of the dance club; we
enjoyed the atmosphere of competitions; and we
especially enjoyed winning a competition.

Was winning our greatest joy?

It was the most intensive experience of joy and
satisfaction that dance sports offered.

What if we didn't win?

This question brings back a memory of a national
championship. We, meaning us and our dance
partner, were favorites because we had won the
previous three or four competitions. But at these
nationals we came only second – and were terribly
disappointed!

Where was our natural joy of moving? When children
move, it's a play.

When ravens fly in circles, it seems to be a play for
them. No raven seems to want to show its skills or
prove its superiority over others. Only for survival it
is important to be faster or stronger than others.

The ability to compare is the very essence of what
distinguishes us from animals and thus makes us
human.[6] Therefore, comparing is part of a person's
curious exploration of the world. For example,
children can only learn that there are different colors
by comparing colors. Naturally, children compare

---

[6] For details, see the book on consciousness.

everything, which includes comparing themselves
with others. A little boy sitting in the bathtub with his
sister will compare himself with her and notice that
their bodies differ. There is no judgement. It's just an
expression of curiosity.

But when we grow up, we learn to judge and to
consider certain things as better than other things.
With this, comparisons lose the innocence of curious
exploration.

Judging leads to the desire to be better. Judging
leads to hierarchies. With this, people turned play
into fights – fights against others and fights against
themselves.

But even in nature there are fights.

Fights in nature have biological purposes. A fight
between predator and prey is about survival – for
both. A fight within a species is about food,
hierarchy, reproduction, or territory. Humans use
fights as a source of satisfaction. This is because we
learn to feel good when we are better than others.

How about the spectators of a sporting fight?

Many spectators take sides. The winner of a sporting
fight experiences personal satisfaction and creates
satisfaction for his or her fans. Athletes get paid for
this directly or indirectly by their fans.

This turned sports into a business.

Because sports create satisfaction, they are an
alternative channel for true curiosity – for athletes
and for fans.

Moving is natural. Sports are a human invention.
Performing a physical sport is a balancing act
between moving, personal growth, distraction, and
satisfaction. It takes a lot of self-honesty to find your
truth in it.

**

With our reflections, no stone is left unturned.

**

What else satisfied us when we grew up?

Intimate encounters.

In other words, *sex*. That's the next alternative
channel for true curiosity.

But sex is natural.

Mating for reproduction is natural. For humans, sex
is much more than mating.

What is sex?

The word *sex* originates from the Latin word *secare*
(= *to divide or cut*). In everyday language, *sex* stands
both for *gender* and *sexual activity.*

Human sex is an extremely complex and subtle topic.
Sex as sexual activity is *communication,* ie a *creation
of togetherness.*

Humans can communicate in a lot of ways – through words, through touch, …

The big question regarding sex is: What makes a communication a sexual communication? Everyone has their view …

… because everyone has their attitude on sex.

For many people, sex is a loaded or distressing topic because they have had traumatic sexual experiences. Sex is one of the most sensitive human topics.

What is sex for *us*?

Communication with emphasis on the curious exploration of a body and its reactions with all senses.

This definition leaves a lot of room for curiosity.

Giacomo Casanova thought so:

Love is three quarters curiosity.
(Giacomo Casanova)

We believe Casanova was referring to the physical aspect of love, ie lovemaking or sex.

How can sex be an alternative channel for curiosity if it expresses curiosity?

Sex *can* express curiosity. But most people don't have truly curious sex.

How do we know?

From experience and from research. First, most
people are not *with* their sex partner during sex,
which contradicts the meaning of the word
communication.

Even in non-intimate communications, such as
conversations, many people are not *with* their
conversation partners and barely listen to them.
Instead, they focus on what they want to say next.
Many conversations are but fights for speaking time.

Most people use intimacy to act out their sexual
fantasies, which are often based on romantic or
pornographic templates. Most people have goal-
driven sex, such as wanting physical satisfaction.

Another goal of sex can be power and control –
either the exercise of power, or the experience of
powerlessness. And, last but not least, many people
perform sex to experience an orgasm.

Isn't an orgasm just the culmination of physical
satisfaction?

An orgasm is more than that. The French paraphrase
"la petite mort" means *"the little death."* An orgasm
is experienced as a dissolution of the self, ie the
vanishing of one's separation from everything else.
When the self dissolves, all difficulties and problems
dissolve – at least for a short while.

An orgasm can be an escape.

For some people, a sexual encounter is a distraction
from everyday life – a kind of sport.

Ultimately, most people perform sex by copying
what they have heard from others, read in books or
articles, or seen in films. Truly curious sex is an
adventure. It is an exploration without templates and
goals.

What about tantric sex?

Tantra and Kamasutra are programs and therefore
have nothing to do with true curiosity. As soon as
you use a book, a film, or a seminar as a template,
you copy – instead of exploring curiously. Even
copying your own truly curious exploration from a
few days ago is no expression of true curiosity.

Sex is a complex and subtle topic.

Pretty much everything people practice as sex today
is not truly curious sex, but a means to experience
sexual pleasure or satisfaction, to act out fantasies,
to exercise power, to experience powerlessness, to
distract yourself, or to enjoy personal dissolution for
a few seconds. For most people, sex is an alternative
channel for true curiosity.

What does it take for truly curious sex between two
people?

It takes two people who are truly curious about each
other, truly like each other, trust each other, have
none of the above motives, and engage in an aimless
exploration of their bodies together.

Sounds exciting!

Besides food, sex is the other topic that plays a
paramount role in our society. Sex is in many ways
like food. Some people crave quantity, meaning
frequent and long sex. Other people crave variety,
meaning changing sexual practices or sex partners.

**

The three geniuses Einstein, Picasso, and Tesla are
men. Proportionally, there are fewer women who
left comparatively lasting marks in the recorded
history.

Which is not to say that there were not many women
who contributed significantly. Historians may have
ignored them.

Is there a difference between men and women in
terms of true curiosity?

No. Girls are just as curious as boys from birth. But
there is a gender difference in the way society
suppresses and diverts true curiosity. This affects
girls more than boys. Therefore, boys have a *slightly*
higher chance of retaining *some* of their curiosity
when growing up.

When we grew up, it was common to give gender-
specific gifts. Boys got building sets, model cars, and
toy trains. Girls got dolls and dollhouses.

That has changed as awareness of gender equality
grew.

**

The alternative channels we looked at so far use natural physical impulses. Eating is based on the natural hunger for food. Collecting is partially based on the desire to grasp. Sports are based on the hunger for moving. Sex is partially based on the animal mating program. The next topic is subtle. The next alternative channel for curiosity is information.

What do we mean by this?

It is what is usually called 'knowledge.' But in truth it is only 'information,' for we already explored the original meaning of the word knowledge.

Is this about what one learns from books, lectures, etc?

Yes, but not only. It's about *gossip, news,* and *expert information.*

Gossip is information about what other people do. Who loves whom? Who fights whom? Who has what disease? Who earns how much? Who goes on vacation where? Who bought what car? And so on. Focus is on family, friends, neighbors, etc, ie people from one's social groups. These people are also the channels that spread this information.

Practically everyone takes part. Some more, some less, some only sporadically; but ultimately everyone.

When family members talk about Aunt Margaret's illness or Cousin Tom's new car, it's gossip. This information is irrelevant to your life, but it can evoke distressing feelings such as pity, fear, envy, anger,

mischievousness. Apart from that, dealing with it
costs precious lifetime.

> Media use gossip about the man in the streets for
> their business. They satisfy interest in people's lives
> with talk shows, courtroom shows, and many other
> variations of reality TV.

There is also gossip about celebrities. The topics are
the same as above, but the focus is on people who
are in the media spotlight, such as actors, athletes,
and politicians.

> Media creates celebrities and also disseminates
> gossip about them.

Media also disseminates *news*. This is information
about what happened where in politics, business,
sports, etc.

> Virtually everyone consumes news via television,
> newspapers, or the internet.

But this information, too, is irrelevant for your life.
This information, too, can create distressing feelings.
And consuming news also costs precious lifetime.

> People believe it is important to know what is
> happening where on this planet.

Because they are conditioned to believe so. It's like
with mealtimes. A few hundred years ago, people
didn't have the means to know what happens or
happened just a few miles away – and they lived
their lives well.

> Are there any news that is important?

What news would that be? Who was or was not
elected president? Who won a championship? None
of applies to your life.

What about news about natural disasters or terrorist
attacks? What if we plan a trip?

This question is inspired by fear. If something is
important, we will get to know even if we don't
consume news regularly. We could check the news
when planning or before going on a trip.

What about serious expert information?

What do we mean by this?

Information obtained from schools, universities,
lectures, seminars, nonfiction books, or professional
journals.

These channels disseminate information about the
perspectives of people who are called experts. True
curiosity is not interested in people's perspectives,
because true curiosity is autonomous.

Einstein could have read about space and time. But
he was truly curious, so he explored space and time
himself. Those who are satisfied with what they hear
or read are not truly curious.

Is this independent of the quality of the source?

All people have just perspectives. There is no
authority that can be trusted unconditionally. Even
the great Sir Isaac Newton, who was considered the
Pope of physics for centuries, was wrong about the
nature of space and time.

A truly curious person questions what he or she
reads or hears and searches for answers themselves.

That's what Einstein did. He read the publications of
other scientists not to find answers, but to get ideas
for his research.

People who refer to the latest scientific findings ...

... demonstrate that they are not truly curious.

We can hear the protest of the "smart people" like
scientists, researchers, academics, ...

... and all others who have invested a lot of time and
money in education and training. We would have
protested a few years ago. But after years of
explorations and research, we have new perspectives
on a lot of issues.

It is what it is. In science there is a lot of arrogance
and misunderstandings about knowledge and truth.
We *may* say that because we worked for years as a
scientist at a university and performed
internationally leading research in two research
areas. We speak from experience. Science is a
fraternity that has its rules.

Einstein's experience is a splendid example.

After graduation, he could not find a job at any
university in Europe. This was because he had the
reputation of questioning established results and
performing unorthodox research. In other words:
Einstein did not find employment because he was
truly curious. Some well-meaning professors had
warned him that his behavior would be bad for his

career. But Einstein remained true to himself and
performed his research privately. Thanks to
fortunate circumstances, his articles were published
in the prestigious journal *"Annalen der Physik,"* and
things went from there.

One of the greatest science geniuses of all times
could not gain a foothold in the scientific
establishment and had to pursue his research
privately. It was only after the value of his private
research has become apparent that he was
recognized in academic circles. This provides ample
food for thought.

Information obtained from books or teachers is only
an alternative channel for true curiosity.

People may have attended many schools and
universities, earned multiple academic degrees, and
read hundreds of books. All this may "feel good," but
all they really know is who has had what perspective.

This is not only the case in academia.

It's the same in spiritual circles. Most spiritual people
refer to ancient traditions that are defined by ancient
texts …

… such as the Bible and the Vedas.

People in spiritual circles read and study texts and
quote masters. But virtually none of them knows =
sees for themselves.

We've had this experience. We talked to a representative of a Buddhist center about our research about the soul. But none of what he said came from him. He only quoted books and masters. It was impossible to have a truly curious conversation.

Questioning the tradition is taboo in these circles. Questioning Buddha or Jesus is unthinkable. True curiosity is not to be found there.

Would one actually question, for example, Buddha?

True curiosity questions *everything*. Einstein questioned the teachings of Newton, the Pope of physics. Buddha cannot be questioned because he is dead, and no one knows what he *really* has said or taught. Buddhists refer to what Buddha allegedly has said and taught. Their major source is the Pali Canon, the most complete surviving canon of early Buddhism. However, each text is only a shadow of what inspired the author to say or write it. The most beautiful love poem is only a shadow of the love experience that inspired it. The Pali Canon dates from 29 BCE, which is about 450 years after the death of Gautama Buddha. This means that Buddha's teachings were passed down partly orally for 450 years. Anyone who has played a game of telephone knows what oral transmission can do to content. Copying or translating texts into other languages may also result in changes to the content.

**

The next alternative channel for true curiosity is travel. This subject is even more subtle than the subject of information.

Let's begin with finding out what the word *travel*
means – as well as the synonyms *journey* and
voyage.

> The word *travel* originates from the Old French word
> *travail* (= *work, labor, arduous journey*).

> The word *journey* originates from the Old French
> word *journée* (= *a day's length; day's work or travel*).

> The word *voyage* originates from the Latin word
> *viaticum* (= *a journey; provisions for a journey*), which
> has the Latin root *via* (= *road, journey, travel*). The
> word *via* has the PIE root *wegh-* (= *to go, move*).

The essence of travel is *motion*. Every motion is a
change. The desire to travel is a desire for *change*.

> Thus travel expresses true curiosity because change
> brings something new.

Not necessarily, because you could walk in circles –
or go back to something old.

Travel *can* express true curiosity. However, for most
people it is a compensation for changes that would
be necessary in other areas of life.

> So, when someone is dissatisfied with their familiar
> life, they develop a desire for change. But instead of
> changing what needs to be changed, they go on a
> voyage. This voyage becomes a temporary escape
> from their dissatisfaction with their life – a kind of
> symptomatic treatment.

Even more so because most voyages are *vacations*, ie
off-duty time.

Since the core of the familiar life is the place of
residence, travel is a very efficient method of escape.
Most travels on this planet are but temporary
escapes from familiar lives.

> For these people, travel is not about *"visiting the
> new"* but *"escaping the old."*

Do animals travel?

> Basically, an animal stays in its territory. A territory is
> an area that feeds it. When a territory no longer
> feeds an animal, it finds a new one. A change of
> territory can be temporary, such as a place to spend
> the winter, or be permanent, such as after a wildland
> fire.
>
> Animals migrate only when circumstances force
> them. How does this insight apply to humans?

We humans, too, are fed by a place. Since we need
both physical and mental food, we need a place that
feeds us both physically and mentally. Supermarkets
and global trade make most food available almost
everywhere, almost anytime. Therefore, above all,
we need a place that feeds us mentally. An apt word
for this is *inspiration*. We need a place that inspires
us.

> Picasso moved to Paris when he was 21 because the
> city inspired him.

Later in his career, Picasso occasionally traveled to
other places to find additional inspiration. Usually he
spent months in these places – and his artistic tools
were always with him. Several times, such voyages
started new artistic phases or gave birth to new art
styles.

It is an art to know, where the right place to live is,
when to move to a new place, and when to travel to
which place for additional inspiration. When a place
"calls," you should go.

Today, most people plan their voyages months in
advance.

Almost every voyage that is planned months in
advance is a planned escape from the familiar life.
Appetite works only in the present.

There is an inn with ten guestrooms near where we
live. The inn is fully booked for the Christmas
holidays of the next three years. All these bookings
are from regular guests.

This shows that for some people travel is a habit. And
habit is the opposite of curiosity.

There are people for whom travel is an important
means of living out their true curiosity. A prime
example was the German naturalist Alexander von
Humboldt, one of the last great universal scholars.
His curiosity reached into many scientific fields
including physics, chemistry, geology, mineralogy,
volcanology, botany, zoology, oceanography,
climatology, and astronomy. Humboldt undertook
several research voyages, more aptly called
expeditions. The Spanish-American expedition, for
example, lasted over five years. On his expeditions
he observed, measured, collected, and documented.

Also today there are people who travel for such
reasons and thus out of true curiosity. Examples
include oceanographers and climate scientists.

Travel may also be necessary in other professions. A salesperson may need to travel to a customer. A scientist may need to travel to a conference.

Traveling can have different motives:
• Traveling to a place that inspires you expresses true curiosity.
• Traveling to explore the world expresses true curiosity.
• Traveling to a place to do your job is a professional necessity.
• Traveling to escape your familiar life is an alternative channel for true curiosity.

The latter accounts for the overwhelming majority of travel on this planet. As with sports, it needs a lot of self-honesty to find the truth in your travels.

Mass tourism shows a global dissatisfaction of people with their lives.

On long weekends, endless streams of traffic roll down the highways. Countless people take *every* opportunity to escape their homes.

Since home is the center and symbol of one's familiar life, this means that countless people want to escape their familiar life.

But they are creatures of habit who also want to keep their familiar lives.

They want to keep their familiar life *and* escape from it. That's preposterous!

We see and understand it because we've researched it meticulously. But people don't see the big picture –

how could they? They experience stress and desire
and deal with it the way they've learned to deal with
it: eat, collect, exercise, have sex, consume
information, travel to other places, etc. But whatever
they do has only a short-term effect.

**

Are there other alternative channels?

Drugs. Caffeine and sugar; alcohol and nicotine;
intoxicants such as marijuana (hashish), LSD, heroine,
and synthetic drugs.

**

Behind these alternative channels are industries that
serve and profit from them.

These industries make a huge part of the global
economy.

And, for most people, these alternative channels
make a huge part of their lives.

The lives of truly curious people consist mostly of
their truly curious pursuits – play, research, art,
inventing, etc.

8

What if a child would fully develop its craving for
comprehending and creating?

It would become a brilliant adult of at least the
caliber of Einstein, Picasso, or Tesla.

To understand this answer, we look at the
development of curiosity step by step.

We start with the craving for food and moving. What
would happen if a child didn't get food?

It would starve to death.

What if the child couldn't move?

Its locomotor system would atrophy – and thus it
would die as well.

Next is the craving for grasping. What if the child
couldn't grasp anything? Say, the parents tied the
child's hands or removed all objects from its
environment.

The child would not learn to grasp. The motility of its
hands would remain undeveloped.

The third step is the craving for naming. What if no
one spoke to the child? No one named the objects it
points to?

The child would not learn to name objects. It would
not learn to speak.

The child's voice would remain undeveloped. If it
doesn't learn to name objects, it doesn't learn to
speak a language. It could not think and
communicate how we think and communicate,
because this is based on spoken language.

The fourth step is the craving for comprehending,
which makes the child ask countless 'why' questions.
We assume the child is well nourished and can move,
grasp and speak, but it may not play and no one
answers its questions.

The child would not learn to comprehend.

The fifth step is the craving for creating. Say, the
child must not build anything or draw pictures.

The child would not learn to create.

The child's mind would remain undeveloped because
comprehending and creating develop the mind.

We say *"would,"* but this happens, though not so
drastically. Children may play, but they are often
interrupted – such as with *"lunch is ready."* Children
may build and paint, but they are often corrected –
such as with *"a sun is not blue and the cow's head is
too big."* Children are conditioned to copy reality –
instead of being truly creative. True curiosity goes
beyond what is, beyond reality.

Picasso was a child prodigy. His creativity was
curtailed when he was trained in the tradition of
nineteenth-century painting by his father, who was a
painter and art teacher. But Picasso had the courage
to break free. He left his family and Spain and moved
to Paris. There he worked intensively to free himself
from his conditionings.

According to US-American writer Gertrude Stein, who was friends with Picasso and knew him very well, Picasso was *"possessed by the necessity of emptying himself."*

It took me four years to paint like Raphael,
but a lifetime to paint like a child.
(Pablo Picasso)

Those who don't follow Picasso's example of freeing themselves from their programs inevitably remain curtailed.

A few years ago, we realized this. Accepting it was anything but easy. But it was the prerequisite to change it.

The uncomfortable truth is: The minds of practically all adults are only rudimentarily developed.

But there were and are many successful people who have done or are doing great things. That doesn't look like the result of underdeveloped minds.

Is 200 pounds light or heavy?

We cannot answer this question.

Why not?

Because light and heavy require a reference. 200 pounds is heavy compared to 100 pounds, but light compared to 300 pounds.

A person who weighs 200 pounds is a heavyweight
among jockeys because a jockey must not weigh over
130 pounds. But among sumo wrestlers, a
200-pound person is a lightweight.

           So, people are more like jockeys than sumo wrestlers
           in terms of mental skills?

Albert Einstein seems the pinnacle of what the
human mind is capable of, ...

           ... but he could as well be the proverbial one-eyed
           man who is king among the blind.

           What would people be capable of if they fully
           developed their mental faculties?

Then Einstein, Picasso, and Tesla would not be the
peak but the valley of what is possible for humans.

           Do adults in all cultures treat their children like we
           do? What about indigenous people?

Indigenous people also condition their children
through example and education. They have their
variant of the human program.

**

What is needed for hand motility to develop fully?

           It needs objects that challenge the hand motor skills.

In a world comprising only large round stones, a child
cannot fully develop its hand motility …

> … because in such a world it doesn't *need* a fully
> developed hand motility.

What does a child need in order to develop a voice
and a language?

> It needs people who speak the language in the child's
> presence – provided the child has healthy hearing.

A child learns the language it hears spoken. It learns
the language to the extent it is spoken. American
English yields American English. British English yields
British English. An English vocabulary with only 300
words yields an English vocabulary with only 300
words.

> Is there an upper limit?

No. When a child grows up in an environment with
three languages, it will learn all three languages.

We once met a family with an Austrian mother, a
Hungarian father, and two daughters who were born
and raised in England, so they spoke English fluently.
The family moved from England to Austria, where
the mother gave birth to a third child, a son. The
mother spoke German with the boy, the father
Hungarian, and the two sisters English. The boy
learned all three languages.

What is needed for a child to develop its mental
abilities?

It needs people with developed mental abilities who challenge the child mentally.

A child's mind develops as permitted by its environment.

The apple doesn't fall far from the tree.

In every respect.

What role does curiosity play?

It plays a key role. True curiosity is the driving force that makes us permanently crave for new experiences so that we can grow mentally.

True curiosity permanently wants to comprehend *more* and create *more*.

We are familiar with what we know. True curiosity makes us want the unknown.

Which often requires leaving the known.

What happens when we find something unknown?

We deal with it. We explore it. We investigate it. We gain experience.

What happens with the unknown?

We get to know it.

What does true curiosity do to us then?

It urges us to find something unknown again. But this
goes on and on … when does it stop?

That's a good question. When does it stop?

Never.

True curiosity has no goal and is never done.

I always do that which I cannot do,
in order that I may learn how to do it.
(Pablo Picasso)

**

What is *evolution*?

This word originates from the Latin roots *ex* (= *out*)
and *volvere* (= *to roll*). An evolution is a *"rolling out."*
It is related to the word *develop*, which originates
from the Old French words *des* (= *undo*) and *veloper*
(= *to wrap up*). An evolution is an outward motion.

Is the direction important?

An inward motion is limited because the inside is
limited. An outward motion is unlimited. An inward
motion necessarily has a goal, an outward motion
needs no goal.

The growth of a plant can be considered a "rolling
out."

In biology, the word *evolution* refers to the
*"development of lower to higher organized life
forms."* Colloquially, it denotes the big picture of the
emergence of species on this planet. But also the
development of a single living being is an evolution in
the genuine sense of the word.

We looked at the evolution of our son, …

… which helped us understand how the three
primary human tools – hands, voice, and mind –
develop in parallel with curiosity.

Humans have a physical component and a mental
component. Therefore, they undergo both a physical
and a mental evolution.

An evolution is a motion. Behind every motion is a
mover, ie a motor. The hunger for food and moving
is the motor of a person's physical evolution.

Therefore, mental hunger (true curiosity) is the
motor of a person's mental evolution.

It makes a difference whether a person lives out its
true curiosity as Einstein, Picasso, and Tesla did, or
whether the power behind it flows in alternative
channels.

People who try to satisfy their mental hunger with
physical food will not grow mentally, …

… but physically beyond the norm. Likewise,
collecting/possessing/shopping, sex, and sports don't
bring mental growth either.

One may assume that information and travel help
mental development.

Information only creates an "inner library." For
knowledge and comprehension – and thus mental
growth – you must see for yourself.

Tourist travel doesn't bring mental growth either
because it is just an escape from familiar life.

A person can grow mentally only through curious
explorations of the world.

Almost each of us carries a memory of deep joy in
and satisfaction with life. It is what we experienced
as a child – provided our biological needs were
satisfied and we could curiously explore the world.

Because of this memory, we feel the longing to
experience it again.

But nothing of what we've learned to do, neither
eating, nor collecting, nor sports, nor sex, nor
information, nor travel, nor drugs brings this
satisfaction. Therefore, we keep searching.

9

With our insights into hunger for life, we should have an answer to one of the greatest questions: What is the meaning of life?

Before we look at the *meaning* of life, we must understand *life*.

Life is what is in us.

This answer is correct, but useless. A useful answer is: life is the prevention of death.

Sounds dramatic.

Put less dramatically: life is the prevention of decay. Everything in the universe decays, ie falls apart. Leaves wither. Meat rots. Stones decay to sand. Even stars eventually collapse into a white dwarf, a neutron star, or a black hole.

We talked about decay in connection with an unused locomotor system. The degeneration (decay) of muscles can be prevented by training, ie by work.

In physics, 'work' equals 'force times distance.' So, a force enables something to remain what it is. *This* is the principle of life.

The word *life* originates from the PIE root *leip-* (= *to stick, adhere*). When we stick something together, it remains together. Life is what remains.

For something to remain what it is, a force must be
applied, ie work must be performed. Life must make
an effort to stay alive.[7]

> There must be a force "behind" life, which makes
> this possible. We call it *life force*.

We've asked before what moves life and creates
behavior. We had called this mover *hunger for life*.
The Latin word for mover is *motor*. Motors are
power sources. So, hunger for life must be a power
source.

> This completes a chain of thought. Hunger for life is
> the power source from which the life force emerges.

Curiosity is mental hunger (for life). Therefore,
curiosity is a person's mental power source. It brings
forth a person's mental life force.

> A person is as alive as he or she is truly curious.

**

Health and illness are closely linked to life.

> What's the role of illness?

What is illness?

---

[7] We discuss the five principles of life in the book on consciousness.

The opposite of health.

What is health? What does the word health mean?

It has the PIE root *kailo-* (= *whole*).

A living being is healthy when it is whole, ie when it
lives up to its whole (full) potential.

This reminds us of the ravens that flew in majestic
circles. They seemed in full possession of their flying
skills. They were healthy.

How about the following image of life: Life plays out
between two extreme states: health and death. We
imagine a river that rises in a spring and ends in a
waterfall. The spring represents health, the waterfall
represents death, and the river represents natural
decay. Life is like swimming in this river.

This image illustrates why life has to make an effort
to stay alive. Without the right effort, we inevitably
move downstream towards the waterfall = death.

Moving is not enough to stay alive. We must swim
against the current, ie against decay. When we swim
with the current, we also move, but we even speed
up decay.

Stress and burnout come to mind.

A living being must permanently make an effort to
stay alive. It must permanently work toward health,
ie swim toward the spring.

How do you swim toward the spring?

By developing your potential and living up to it at the highest level. Every wild animal does this. Therefore, birds fly for the sake of flying and sing for the sake of singing.

Every animal develops its sensorimotor skills and then maintains them at the highest level – thus keeping itself healthy and competitive.

This is comparable to a world-class athlete. The athlete must first work hard (train) to reach world-class level and then continue to train to maintain the level. Working less hard leads to a weakening of the skills – and loss of competitiveness.

The weakening of skills is natural decay.

A healthy person (in the genuine sense of the word) is someone who lives up to his or her full (highest) physical *and* mental potential. However, there is virtually no one on this planet who does this.

What about the three geniuses?

All three had lived up to only part of their potential. Through unhealthy lifestyles, they used up their physical reserves early on.

Although Picasso smoked like a chimney and drank like a fish, he lived to be 91.

This seems remarkable, but we've already asked if 200 pounds is light or heavy. 91 years is a "nice age" by the usual standards, and Picasso owes it to the fact that he lived up to much of his artistic potential. But 91 years of life may be little compared to what is possible for humans.

Back to the question: What role does illness play?

If we understand illness as symptoms that limit the
quality of life, it is a sign. It reminds us that life
naturally moves downstream toward death. It
reminds us that we need to take responsibility for
our life and our health.

This does not mean popping pills.

Most medical therapies try to suppress symptoms.
But even naturopathy does not dig deep enough for
the actual causes.

We experienced this at the age of 25.

We suffered from a chronic, very painful pharyngitis.
In search of a cure, we spent five months going from
doctor to doctor. Therapies ranged from antibiotics
to throat rinses, but all to no avail. Our throat
remained inflamed, was fiery red, and every
swallowing hurt. The fifth doctor was an internist.
After a major medical check, which remained
without findings, he said: *"I don't know what's wrong
with you. Try vitamin pills. They may help."*

Until that day, we had a blind faith in science and
rejected alternative treatments such as homeopathy
as unproven nonsense. But since scientific medicine
had failed on us, in desperation we consulted a
natural healer. He diagnosed a kidney inflammation
and prescribed a homeopathic remedy. When we
told him we had come for a sore throat, he explained
that the kidneys are part of the immune system and
because of the kidney situation, the immune system
couldn't cope with the throat situation. To our
surprise, the therapy worked. Our throat "healed" —
ie it became symptom free.

This was great. But ultimately, this was just symptom treatment, albeit at a physically deeper level than what scientific medicine had tried. The next question would have been: *Why* are the kidneys inflamed?

> How deep do you have to look for the cause of an illness?

At the deepest causal level, every illness is a reminder to live up to your highest potential. This is the only path to true health.

> How do we know?

From experience. Since 2011, we meticulously explore ourselves. During these years, an intensive dialogue between "us" and our body has developed. We've gained a lot of experience regarding the connections between thinking, feeling, and body.

> So the meaning of life is to develop your physical and mental abilities at the highest level?

Yes. You can also put it this way: The meaning of life is to live up to your full (highest) potential. Every animal, every plant, and every cell on this planet does it.

**

> We've been asked several times if we've found peace or happiness through exploring consciousness and ourselves. This reflects the widespread belief that the meaning of life is to reach a state of peace or happiness.

The word *state* shows that there is something wrong
with this. Motion is a characteristic of life. A state is
the opposite of motion and therefore cannot express
life. Our picture of life as a river makes this clear.
Without the right motion, you are inevitably moving
toward death.

Let's consider happiness. Happiness exists only as the
opposite of unhappiness. One can experience both
only in mutual alternation.

> Happiness needs unhappiness to be experienced as
> happiness.

Conversely, unhappiness needs happiness to be
experienced as unhappiness. Permanent happiness
does not exist, nor does permanent unhappiness.

> It's like mountains and valleys. They also "need" each
> other. A permanent mountain is as impossible as a
> permanent valley.

> Is there permanent peace?

There is nothing permanent in the universe. The
essence of the universe is change, because in the
universe everything moves/changes.

> Therefore, eternal peace, as desired by so many
> people, is a pipe dream.

The word *peace* has the PIE root **pag-* (= *to fasten*).
This is the opposite of change/growth and thus the
opposite of life. Peace exists only as or in death.
Therefore, many tombstones bear the text *"Rest in
Peace."*

Most spiritual people strive for peace.

They do everything to find peace. But with this they
strive for the opposite of life – without knowing =
seeing it.

Their quest for peace is one reason why so many
spiritual people end up in illness. On the one hand,
they seek peace, which is the opposite of life. On the
other hand, their seeking expresses their desire to
receive answers – even if they are not aware of their
questions. We know this from experience. We were
on a spiritual path for years – and only got sick and
sicker.

Illness is an answer. It's the body's reminder to
develop your potential to the highest level – to swim
upstream to the source.

Not just spiritual people seek peace. All people do,
though they may call it something else, such as
"happiness" or *"being done."*

Peace, happiness, and being done have nothing to do
with life and health – on the contrary.

Thus, people are running after the wrong goals.

People do what they have learned to do.

**

We mess with everyone!

We say what we've found out and experienced.
Einstein, Picasso, and Tesla also called a spade a
spade.

Do we compare ourselves with these three geniuses?

We must, because we take ourselves seriously.

Taking oneself seriously is different from taking
oneself important, as is widespread among people.

Every child is a genius.

The word *genius* is Late Latin and means *"talent."* A
genius is a person with talent.

Every child is naturally talented, because it has the
power of true curiosity. Since this power, and thus
genius, can be diverted but not destroyed, there is
genius in every person, regardless of age.

Therefore, there is genius in us as well. We compare
ourselves with the three geniuses because we are
truly curious and courageous and reach for the stars.

We can reach the stars only when we reach for them.
Einstein, Picasso, and Tesla also had reached for the
stars. All children do – until they are programmed
that they are too small to reach them.

In his autobiography, Tesla gave a vivid example. He
wrote about the physics course he had taken at the
Polytechnic University in Graz, Austria:

*"I made a remark that it might be possible to use
such a motor without the collectors. But Professor*

*Pöschl explained that this was not possible, and he
gave me a proper lesson, at the end of which he said:
'Mister Tesla may achieve great things, but he will
never achieve this. That would be like converting a
force of attraction, such as gravity, into an angular
momentum. That's an idea for a perpetuum mobile, a
physical impossibility.' "*

A few years later, Tesla had the idea for this *"physical
impossibility:"* He invented the alternating current
generator and thus laid the foundation for the
modern global electricity system.

> Good thing Tesla didn't let his professor discourage
> him.

Like so many, we too were discouraged at a young
age. We remember the following episode:

We were ten or eleven years old. It was a Sunday
evening. The family was driving home after visiting
relatives. We thought aloud about how gravity could
be neutralized with a black hole. We had barely
finished the sentence when our mother commented:
*"If it were that easy, other people would have figured
it out by now."*

> Smack! What a juicy mental slap in the face!

It was the death blow to whatever was left of our
true curiosity, which had declared war on gravity that
evening.

**

A question remains: What is the full potential of a human?

First, we must understand the potential of life. The essence of the universe is change. Life is an aspect of the universe and therefore an aspect of change. Since life is the prevention of decay, its essence is the opposite of decay. An apt word for this is growth.

Thus, the potential of every life form is growth. Cells grow in number, plants grow in size and number, animals grow in sensorimotor skills, size, and number.

The laws of nature limit these types of growth. In the book on consciousness, we describe the difference between humans and non-human life forms. The essence of the difference is: All non-human life forms are limited. Humans are unlimited.

Therefore, the potential of humans is unlimited growth.

Since physical growth is limited by the laws of nature, unlimited growth is only possible mentally. This is achieved through curious explorations of the world.

10

How can you live up to your full potential?

We start with the following story:

One day an eagle laid an egg in a chicken coop. The egg hatched, and the newborn eagle learned from the other birds how to live like a chicken. It used its feet to run around; it pecked for food on the ground; when it saw big birds in the sky, it fearfully took refuge in the chicken house. But there was a yearning in it that was particularly strong when it saw the big birds in the sky. This yearning made it seek. It learned from the other birds what to seek and how to seek. But none of what it found satisfied its yearning.

Someone should tell the eagle that it is not a chicken, but an eagle … that it has wings with which it can fly just like the big birds it is afraid of.

This wouldn't help.

Why not?

The eagle has learned to "be" a chicken; it carries a "chicken program" that tells it how to behave under which circumstances. That's all it knows. It feels safe and comfortable "being" a chicken – except for the yearning.

It could attend an eagle seminar to learn to behave like an eagle.

This would not help either. Learning to be an eagle
would install an eagle program, which would overlay
the chicken program. Then the eagle would be an
eagle who believes it is a chicken who has learned
some eagle behavior.

> So, the eagle would be a "wannabe eagle." How
> strange! This would be even more confusing than
> continuing to live as a chicken.

> How can the eagle be what it truly is?

The eagle has to free itself from the chicken
program.

> Why did the eagle mother lay her egg in the chicken
> coop in the first place?

Because she also lives in the chicken coop and
believes she is a chicken. In fact, ALL birds in the
chicken coop are eagles who believe they are
chickens – and this has been so for thousands upon
thousands of years.

> This story is obviously a metaphor for humankind.

The very nature of a human is true curiosity. True
curiosity is our essence, our eagleness. Every child is
living proof. Every child is ravenously curious and
therefore permanently asks 'Why' and 'Why not?'
But when the child grows up, its curiosity gets
diverted into alternative channels.

> How did the "human chicken program" emerge?

A long time ago, *Homo sapiens* started using its mind. With this, a mental evolution began in which humans became their own creators. In thousands upon thousands of years, this evolution created the *human program*. Every human on this planet carries a variant of this program. The human program "contains" thousands of generations of humans in form of countless individual programs that tell us how to behave in which situation. It corresponds to what we had called the *mental world*.

> When looking at humankind, something must have gone wrong.

Nothing has gone wrong, because evolution has no goal.

> But the current situation of humankind seems quite desperate. Aggression and xenophobia increase at an alarming rate – with devastating consequences. Aggression not only leads to violence, misuse, rape, murder, and war, it is also directed against objects (vandalism), non-human life forms (exploitation), and the planet (pollution and exploitation of resources). Many people direct it against themselves (auto-aggression), which shows as accidents and diseases, even suicide.

This can be understood by looking at the evolution of humans as a species of the family of Great Apes, which also includes orangutans, gorillas, bonobos, and chimpanzees. We explain this in our book *"Being Free: Get Out of the Box"* (see chapter "Resources").

The human program evolved through two mechanisms: *self-conditioning* and *mutual conditioning*. Self-conditioning happens when we think or act. Mutual conditioning happens when we perceive people or consume media.

Over thousands of years, the human program
developed through collective self-conditioning and
collective mutual conditioning. All humans who have
ever lived have unwittingly contributed.

> Then all humans living today unwittingly contribute
> to the human program's further development.

People "inherit" the human program from the first
day of their life simply by perceiving people such as
their parents.

> Just like the newborn eagle perceives the other birds
> and thus "inherits" their chicken behavior.

No one can escape. Practically every human carries
the oldest parts of the human program, which go
back to the beginnings of *Homo sapiens*. The
resulting behavior may appear *natural* for humans.
But it is not; it is only *normal*.

> The word *normal* originates from the Latin word
> *norma* (= *rule, pattern*). Something is normal when it
> occurs as a pattern within a group. The word *natural*
> originates from the Latin word *naturalis* (= *by birth*),
> which goes back to *nasci* (= *be born*). Something is
> natural when one is born with it.

Younger parts of the program have spread only
within certain social groups. They appear as cultural,
religious, national, regional, and familial patterns.

The diversion of the power of true curiosity into
alternative channels is part of the human program.

> Why did it become part of the human program?

Because it happened. Since there is no programmer
behind the human program, there is no intention
behind it. Evolution has no goal. Although … when
you look at the origin of *Homo sapiens* as well as at
what we found out about consciousness, the human
program could not have developed in any other
way.[8]

> We could do a thought experiment in which we
> assume there is a programmer.

We could. But the result would only be of theoretical
value.

> This could lead to new insights. So why not?

> Why has the fictitious programmer redirected the
> power of true curiosity?

Because it is not welcome.

> Why is that so?

Because it is egoistic.

> But egoism *is* a terrible quality.

We have been programmed to believe so.
Considering egoism as bad is a human program.
What does the word *egoism* mean?

---

[8] See chapter "Dead End" in our book *"Being Free: Get Out of the Box."*

Ego is Latin for *"I."* Egoism means putting yourself first.

This is not bad. Every animal does it – except mothers when caring for their offspring. Every child does it – until it is conditioned to consider egoism bad.

Egoism is natural.

What is egoism good for?

It is good for survival. It is a prerequisite for living up to your highest potential.

Developing your potential is a lot of work. You need to invest energy. Everyone who has achieved or achieves something extraordinary was or is egoistic. Einstein was egoistic. Picasso was egoistic. Tesla was egoistic. World-class athletes are egoistic. Successful business leaders are egoistic.

Most people consider egoism cute in young children, but undesirable in teenagers and adults.

Because egoism can be a threat.

Why and how?

When it is combined with power.

How does this combination occur?

It is part of the human program. Let's start with the question: What is freedom?

Freedom is the ability to do what you want.

This definition equates freedom with power: I am
free when I can do what I want.

What's wrong with this definition of freedom?

It is a dangerous illusion.

How is it an illusion?

The following quote gives an excellent answer:

Man can do what he wills, but he cannot will what he wills.
(Arthur Schopenhauer)

True freedom is to be free from willing. The above
definition of freedom, however, makes people
believe that freedom is to be free in doing. This belief
distracts them from their unfreedom of willing.

If willing is not free … where does it come from?

It comes from the human program. People want
what they have *learned* to want. They want what
they have been *conditioned/programmed* to want.

For example, we want to eat what we've learned to
want to eat while growing up in Austria. If we'd been
moved to Japan at a young age, we would have
Japanese eating habits today and therefore would
want to eat something different.

This reasoning applies to any behavior.[9]

Consider caricatures. A few strokes in a sketch can
create a recognizable portrait of a person – provided
the sketch shows its characteristic features.

Then our mind autocompletes the picture from
memory.

Our mind *wants* to see the person it knows.

We *want* to behave how we are used to behaving.
We *want* to behave how we've learned to behave.
We *want* what we are familiar with.

Tesla meticulously observed himself for some time.
He wanted to find out why he thought, spoke, and
acted the way he did. At the end of his observation
experiment, he concluded he is an *"automaton:"*

*In the course of time it became perfectly evident to me
that I was merely an automaton endowed with
the power of movement, responding to the stimuli of the sense
organs and thinking and acting accordingly.
(Nikola Tesla)*

Today we would call this a *robot*.

What a deeply disturbing insight!

____

[9] See chapter "Programs" in our book *"Being free: Get Out of the Box."*

In our exploration of consciousness and the question
'What am I?', we found that people still have a grain
of freedom. The human program controls people
"only" 99.xy%.

> This means that people have less than 1% true
> freedom – with this number decreasing because the
> human program constantly grows.

> Humans are on autopilot most of the time.

Accepting this is the key to changing it.[10]

> We called the above definition of freedom not only
> illusionary but also *dangerous*. How dangerous is it?

This definition of freedom makes people *exercise*
power.

> So it is not enough for them to *have* power. They
> want to *exercise* it.

People don't get satisfaction from *having* power.
Having power is not experienced as freedom.

> Which is logical, because power as freedom is an
> illusion.

Since people don't experience freedom by *having*
power, they try to experience freedom by *exercising*
power.

---

[10] We elaborate on this in our book *"Being Free: Get Out of the Box."*

So, the above definition of freedom is an indirect conditioning to exercise power.

Exercising power leads to power struggles. Let's look at the following example:

Imagine a tree casting a shadow on a house with two apartments. The resident of the one apartment likes the shadow, the resident of the other apartment dislikes it. The one resident wants to keep the tree while the other wants to cut it down. Obviously, only one of them can exercise his or her power. The result is a power struggle.

In the past, power struggles were fought with fists. Today, there are less violent methods, such as democracy and money. But power struggles remain power struggles.

The above definition of freedom creates a power hierarchy within any social group. Those with more power oppress those with less power.

But most people don't seem to fight each other.

Somebody may have power regarding some issues, but be powerless regarding other issues. Therefore, hierarchies vary depending on the issue. This can lead to complex situations in any social group – starting with small groups like partnerships.

How can you become free from willing?

By becoming free from the human program.

The eagle experiences true freedom after it has freed
itself from the chicken program.

There is no social awareness of this form of freedom.

Because people are not aware of their unfreedom of
wanting/willing. They are not aware of being 99% on
autopilot.

This illusory idea of freedom is deeply rooted in
people. It has been part of the human program for a
long time. At the beginning of the twentieth century,
the occultist Aleister Crowley boosted this definition.
He founded a religion/philosophy named *Thelema*.
Thelema is the Latin transliteration of the Greek
word for 'will.' Crowley formulated one fundamental
principle of Thelema: *"Do what thou wilt shall be the
whole of the Law."*

The phrase *"Do what thou wilt"* is a call to exercise
power.

Artists popularized Aleister Crowley and his mindset.
His portrait or name can be found on record covers
of popular musicians and bands such as Michael
Jackson and the Beatles. The above "law" can also be
found in whole or in parts in song lyrics.

Let's remember that this was only a thought
experiment. In the course of our conversation, the
programmer turned into 'the society.' But there is no
society as a controlling entity behind the human
program. The human program evolved in countless

small steps, which accumulated over thousands of
years – without a programmer.

However, throughout history there have been people
who understood the principles of human
programming and used them to their advantage.

This was an enlightening exercise.

**

We've seen that true curiosity is the key to
experiencing true joy in and satisfaction with life.
How can you be truly curious again?

By truly curiously exploring the question: What am I?

This sounds like an impossible task, a "mission
impossible." You need what you want in order to get
it. It's like if a safe key was locked inside the safe.

People are 99 (or more) percent controlled by their
programs. Therefore, they still have up to 1% true
freedom.

Are we saying that a small part of the safe key is
outside the safe and it can open the safe?

Yes. But it's work. Most of your true curiosity is
blocked by the human program. Therefore, the
method is to master the human program. When you
are the master of your prison's key, the prison is not
a prison anymore.

How can you achieve this mastership?

You start with the decision to attain mastership. This decision must come from the true curiosity that is contained in the up to 1% of your true freedom. You use this true curiosity to focus on exploring the question: What am I?

To do this, it helps to understand the mental mechanisms behind the human program.[11]

How is the question 'What am I?' explored?

By observing and exploring your body states, thoughts, feelings, and actions and their connections.[12]

How are answers obtained?

By observing and listening.

The ingredients for success are: seriousness, courage, perseverance, patience, discipline, focus, and egoism.

What is the role of egoism?

It is the basis. Freeing yourself from your programs is an inner struggle in which 1% true curiosity must prevail against 99% human program. After some time it's 2% against 98% ... then 3% against 97% ... and so on.

---

[11] We described them in the book on consciousness.

[12] We describe the method of freeing yourself from your programs in our book *"Being free: Get Out of the Box – The Method with 99 Exercises"*

Sounds like a David versus Goliath battle – and like a
true adventure, because you don't know what will
come out of it.

You can't know. The eagle has to remove the chicken
program to recognize itself as an eagle.

If I only knew who in fact I am,
I should cease to behave as what I think I am;
and if I stopped behaving as what I think I am,
I should know who I am.
(Aldous Huxley in "Island")

In the language of the eagle metaphor, this is:

"If I only knew that I am an eagle,
I should cease to behave as a chicken;
and if I stopped behaving as a chicken,
I should know that I am an eagle."

By eliminating what you are not,
it remains what you are.

11

Are we done?

Done with what?

With exploring curiosity.

When is a truly curious person done?

Never.

So we can't be done. The curious exploration of the
world has no end …

**

The important thing is not to stop questioning.
Curiosity has its own reason for existing.
(Albert Einstein)

**

Glossary

In the sequel the abbreviation PIE is used for 'Proto-Indo-European.'

******

abstract: Latin *ab* (= *away from*) + *trahere* (= *to draw*)

anxiety: PIE **angh-* (= *tight, painfully constricted*)

ask: PIE **ais-* (= *to wish, desire*)

autonomy: Greek *autos* (= *self*) + *nomos* (= *custom, law*)

comprehend: Latin *com* (= *with, together*) + *prehendere* (= *to catch hold of, seize*)

curiosity: Latin *cura* (= *care*)

develop: Old French *des* (= *undo*) + *veloper* (= *to wrap up*)

ego: (Latin) = *I*

evolution: Latin *ex* (= *out*) + *volvere* (= *to roll*)

focus: (Latin) = *hearth, fireplace; center of activity or energy*

health: PIE **kailo-* (= *whole, uninjured*)

hunger: Old German *hungar* (= *burning sensation*); from PIE **kenk-* (= *to burn*)

initiative: Latin *in* (= *into*) + *ire* (= *to go*)

instinct: Latin *in* (= *into*) + *stinguere* (= *to prick, goad*)

journey: Old French *journée* (= *a day's length, day's work or travel*)

know: PIE **gno-* (= *to know*); synonym *wit* from PIE **weid-* (= *to see*)

leisure: Latin *licere* (= *to be allowed*)

life: PIE **leip-* (= *to stick, adhere*)

mathematics: Greek *mathemata* (= *science*)

mental: Latin *mens* (= *mind*)

monk: Greek *monakhos* (= *solitary*); from *monos* (= *alone*)

natural: Latin *naturalis* (= *by birth*); from *nasci* (= *be born*)

new: PIE **newo-* (= *new*)

normal: Latin *norma* (= *rule, pattern*)

peace: PIE **pag-* (= *to fasten*)

perspective: Latin *per* (= *through*) + *specere* (= *to look at*)

question: Latin *quaerere* (= *to ask, seek*)

risk: Italian *riscare* (= *to run into danger*)

sex: Latin *secare* (= *to divide or cut*)

sport: Old French *desport* (= *pleasure, enjoyment*); from Latin *des* (= *away*) + *portare* (= *to carry*)

theory: Greek *theoria* (= *a looking at, viewing*) + *horan* (= *to see*)

travel: Old French *travail* (= *work, labor, arduous journey*)

truth: PIE **deru-* (= *be firm, solid, steadfast*)

vacation: Latin *vacatio* (= *leisure, freedom, exemption, a being free from duty*); from PIE **eue-* (= *to leave, abandon*)

voyage: Latin *viaticum* (= *a journey; provisions for a journey*); *via* from PIE **wegh-* (= *to go, move*)

Resources

Books:

Consciousness: Its Nature, Purpose, and How to Use It (B Kutzler)

>This book is an instruction manual for yourself. I explain in detail what physical and mental mechanisms are at work in you, what exactly consciousness is, and what the nature of our existence is.

Being Free: Get Out of the Box – The Method With 99 Exercises (B Kutzler)

>You are controlled by countless programs. They create most of your behavior and thinking. They make the box that is a prison for your mind. This workbook contains 99 exercises and detailed instructions on how to get free from your programs and thus leave the box.

Website:

https://www.BernhardKutzler.com/

YouTube Channel:

"Dr Bernhard Kutzler"

Contact:

beingfree@kutzler.com

About the Author

I am a researcher and author with a doctorate in mathematics and trainings in subjects ranging from psychology to nutrition to Ayurveda. I was a successful scientist, teacher, and business leader for over twenty years before I left this career to research human behavior. Since 2011, I am exploring, how we can live up to our highest potential. For this, I explore the programs that control us (the "human box") and how to free ourselves from these programs. For the experiential exploration, I lived for 3.5 years with no social interaction and media consumption between 2015 and 2018.

I document my findings and experiences in my books, my blog, and my YouTube channel (see chapter "Resources").

Acknowledgement

This book originally was published in German. I translated it into English.

**

I am grateful to Hannes Kutzler for designing the cover artwork and to Klaus-Jürgen Kutzler, Verena Brunner, and Allison Paradise for comments on the text.